Praise for
Simple Solutions

"The premise of Schmitt and Perl's book is the need to reduce complex problems to their simplest components, an approach I've seen produce powerful results. Managers at all levels would benefit from applying the principles outlined in this book."
> —Pitt Hyde
> Chairman, AutoZone

"In a complex world, we often complicate things more than necessary and forget that the goal is to do the right things as well as possible. This book is a terrific primer on identifying the right things and getting on with them."
> —John Durrett
> Managing Director, McKinsey and Co., Inc., West Coast

"A powerful and thought-provoking book filled with sound advice that would help the young or the experienced executive understand the importance of management and leadership skills. I wish that I had had a book like *Simple Solutions* to guide me through the transition from athlete to executive."
> —Jerry West
> President of Basketball Operations, Memphis Grizzlies

Simple Solutions

Harness the Power of Passion and Simplicity to Get Results

Tom Schmitt and Arnold Perl

BICENTENNIAL
1807
WILEY
2007
BICENTENNIAL

John Wiley & Sons, Inc.

Published by John Wiley & Sons, Inc., Hoboken, New Jersey.
Published simultaneously in Canada.

For general information on our other products and services or for technical
support, please contact our Customer Care Department within the United States
at (800) 762-2974, outside the United States at (317) 572-3993 or
fax (317) 572-4002.

Wiley also publishes its books in a variety of electronic formats. Some content
that appears in print may not be available in electronic books. For more
information about Wiley products, visit our web site at www.wiley.com.

Library of Congress Cataloging-in-Publication Data:

Schmitt, Thomas, 1965–
    Simple solutions : harness the power of passion and simplicity to get
results / Thomas Schmitt, Arnold Perl.
      p. cm.
    Includes bibliographical references and index.
    ISBN-13: 978-0-470-04818-4 (cloth)
    ISBN-10: 0-470-04818-2 (cloth)
    1. Leadership. 2. Simplicity. 3. Problem solving. 4. Employee motivation.
I. Perl, Arnold, 1939– II. Title.
    HD57.7.S3555   2007
    658.4′092—dc22

                                                              2006019440

Printed in the United States of America.

10 9 8 7 6 5 4 3 2 1

To Petra, my parents Ruth and Arnulf, and my brother Joachim.

—Tom Schmitt

To Mary Lynn and our exceptional children, Stephanie and Jonathan Marks, and Laurie and Jeff Meskin and to our six cherished grandchildren, Rachel, Joshua and Julia Marks, and Hannah, Jake, and Daniel Meskin.

—Arnold Perl

Acknowledgments

Even though the solutions we talk about in this book are simple, the process of getting them into print was not—it took a dedicated team, most of whom took this on as a labor of love secondary to their day jobs.

We are indebted to our core team who stuck with us throughout the process, even when we weren't sure if we'd ever get it finished, much less published. We could not have written this book without Becky Babineaux. Becky's creativity, excellence in writing, and "can-do" attitude took us from start to finish. She truly was our star quarterback throughout this journey. In the last few months as our deadline loomed, a lot of tireless effort and very long weekends went

ACKNOWLEDGMENTS

into the endless rewrites and changes in direction
that go into writing a book. The clear thinking, editing, and facilitation skills of Petra Rees helped us or-
ganize our thoughts and put order into a manuscript
that attempted to combine our thoughts and two
leadership styles. Laura Nevins joined the team in the
second half of the project; her writing and editing expertise, along with her dedication to quality, were
invaluable. Doug Sease, who also joined in the second half, provided the guidance and skills of an experienced, published author and helped the team
navigate the maze of the publishing process. His expertise put into place the framework that sped the
book toward its completion. Susan Patton, a first half
member of the team, helped get the project off the
ground. She and graphic designer Jeff Atnip helped
develop the very first rendition of the balanced leadership scale as a team presentation.

Without the guidance of our agent, Karen Gantz,
we most likely would have given *Simple Solutions* up
as a lost cause. Karen's encouragement, along with
that of communications expert Merrie Spaeth, not
only kept us going, but led us to a preeminent publisher and to a successful partnership with John Wiley
& Sons, Inc. Wiley's team of experts were helpful and
patient as they helped a team of publishing green-
horns muddle through the process of sending the
right files, the right artwork, and the right words.

viii

Acknowledgments

Thank you to Wiley's Matt Holt, Shannon Vargo, Kim Dayman, Kate Lindsay, Heather Kornack, Maureen Drexel, and Wiley's compositor Publications Development Company for leading us through the final steps to publication.

Because both of us have quite demanding day jobs, our dedicated office staffs and assistants were gracious and very willing to help. Thank you to Jan Bryan (Arnold's assistant) and Margie Rhodes and Mindy Coker Lange (Tom's assistants). Jan, Margie, and Mindy kept the lines of communications open, scheduled what seemed like hundreds of teleconferences, emailed reams of drafts, and kept up with the players' phone numbers and e-mail addresses.

Others who provided information and were willing to be interviewed for this project included Larry Cox, president and CEO of the Memphis-Shelby County Airport Authority; John Wood, senior vice president, and Dave Mansell, construction manager, for M.A. Mortenson Construction Co. We also benefited from consulting with writer and speaker Sondra Thiederman, author of *Making Diversity Work*. Dr. Thiederman gave us valuable advice about agent selection, which led us to our partnership with the right publisher.

The ideas and the concepts for *Simple Solutions* didn't just happen—they were developed by us over many years and they were nurtured and inspired by many people.

FROM TOM

I am grateful for the people who have inspired us over the years and have provided the examples of true leadership. First and foremost is Frederick W. Smith, who inspired me by his unparalleled leadership, his business principles, and his unfailing sense of direction. He has provided the template for many successful careers including mine.

I have been fortunate to work for FedEx Services CEO T. Michael Glenn for the past five years. Mike is the absolute master at honing in on critical issues that matter most and I learned from the master.

On the creative "right brain" side, I am forever grateful to those who cracked my "people and passion" side wide open and reinforced the importance of giving: initially Stephanie Spong, and, most profoundly, LeeAnne Cox.

In that spirit, a second thank you to Laura Nevins who knows how to make me laugh.

Most importantly, a special thank you to Petra—my wife, partner, and my rock—who has been by my side for more than half of my life. Thank you for pushing me to be the best I can be and for your thoughtful and invaluable contributions to this book.

FROM ARNOLD

James E. McGehee Jr. has been my mentor, and it was his focus on "four pillars of life"—family, faith, career, and community—that most influenced me toward faith-based and civic leadership positions. Those four pillars have forever shaped my life. They led me to work with the very best: Senior Rabbi Micah Greenstein of Temple Israel, Memphis; Larry Cox, president and CEO of the Memphis-Shelby County Airport Authority; John Moore, president and CEO of the Memphis Regional Chamber; and Kevin Kane, president and CEO of the Memphis Convention & Visitors Bureau. I also am very grateful to my law firm, Ford & Harrison LLP, for all of its support.

A special thank you to my wife Mary Lynn. Her considerable influence changed my life. Without her by my side, my life would have certainly taken a different turn.

Contents

CONTENTS

Foreword

I've known Tom Schmitt and Arnold Perl for a number of years and dealt with them in different ways and in different settings—Tom as a senior executive at FedEx and Arnold in several public and private roles.

These are unique and unusually talented individuals who have collaborated to write this creative book. The synthesis of two disparate management experiences and the molding of common solutions into a winning agenda provide a highly useful work.

At its core, *Simple Solutions* is true to its title. The authors demonstrate conclusively that the proven principles of management and leadership are absolute and, in fact, simple. Moreover, they show through their experiences how they effectively applied these principles to achieve remarkable results in various endeavors.

The reiteration of management and leadership truths in this way provides a practical roadmap for anyone interested in these disciplines. Of particular importance is the focus on balanced effectiveness—a combination of utilitarian managerial tools and effective engagement of teammates to create a passion to succeed. Tom and Arnold show that achieving results and accomplishing goals in modern organizations is highly dependent on striking this balance.

While most management books tacitly reinforce these managerial success factors, few provide the real world context found in *Simple Solutions*. In this regard, the lessons of history concerning successful organizations are clear. Failure most often stems from the ignorance or disregard of the fundamental principles of management and leadership. Tom Schmitt and Arnold Perl have made a great contribution to readers by reminding them of the fundamental actions that avoid such outcomes and, instead, ensure favorable results.

Their disciplined approach to these issues provides a welcome addition to the library of any manager in any field.

FREDERICK W. SMITH
Chairman and CEO FedEx Corporation

About the Authors

TOM SCHMITT

As the Chief Executive Officer and President of FedEx Global Supply Chain Services and Senior Vice President of FedEx Solutions, Tom has responsibility for a wide range of solutions for FedEx customers and internal Sales and Operations divisions across all FedEx operating companies. FedEx Global Supply Chain Services offers a suite of logistics solutions that quickly move goods from one end of the supply chain to the other and helps FedEx customers turn supply chain management into a competitive strategy.

He came to FedEx after an eight-year stint with McKinsey & Co, which advises leading companies on issues of strategy, organization, technology, and operations and is considered to be one of the world's most prestigious consulting firms. Tom's work there with Fortune 500 companies included strategy development and operations efforts for the transportation, logistics, retail, utilities, and telecom industries.

Prior to his time with McKinsey, Tom worked for London-based British Petroleum (BP) where his work included project management and financial analysis for the company's retail marketing network redesign initiative. He later left BP's London headquarters to serve in a line management capacity for BP in Cleveland, Ohio.

Tom was born and raised in Biberach, Germany, and holds degrees from Harvard Business School (MBA with highest distinction) and Middlesex University (B.A. with First Class Honors) in London. Tom serves on the board of LOGTECH, an advisory organization to the Department of Defense, and as an advisory panel member of the Corporate Executive Board. He also serves as a Director on the Executive Board of the Memphis Regional Chamber of Commerce and on the Board of Directors and the Executive Committee for Ballet Memphis.

ARNOLD PERL

Arnold Perl, a partner at the national labor and employment law firm of Ford & Harrison LLP, has been a practicing management attorney for more than 30 years. Arnold has received local, national, and international recognition that includes listings in *The Best Lawyers in America* for more than 20 years, and the *International Who's Who of Management Labour and Employment Lawyers*. He was recognized in *Business Tennessee* Magazine as one of the Top 100 of "Tennessee's Most Powerful People" and named to "Who's Who" in *Memphis Magazine* as one of the Top 100 influential Leaders 2006–2007. Arnold was inducted into the Airport Minority Advisory Council Hall of Fame in 2006 for his efforts to grow airport diversity and was named the 2006 Humanitarian of the Year by Diversity Memphis for his contribution to the promotion of tolerance in the Memphis community.

Arnold serves as Chairman of the Memphis-Shelby County Airport Authority, shaping and directing the decisions of Memphis' economic engine and as Chairman of the New Memphis Arena Public Building Authority, which received great acclaim for overseeing construction of the FedExForum, home of the NBA Memphis Grizzlies. Arnold is counsel to the Memphis Regional Chamber of Commerce. He also is Chairman Emeritus, Japan-America Society of

Tennessee and Chairman Emeritus (Co-Chair), Southeast U.S./Japan Association, as well as Trustee Emeritus, University of Tennessee.

Arnold received the Communicator of the Year Award from the Public Relations Society of America (Memphis chapter, 2005).

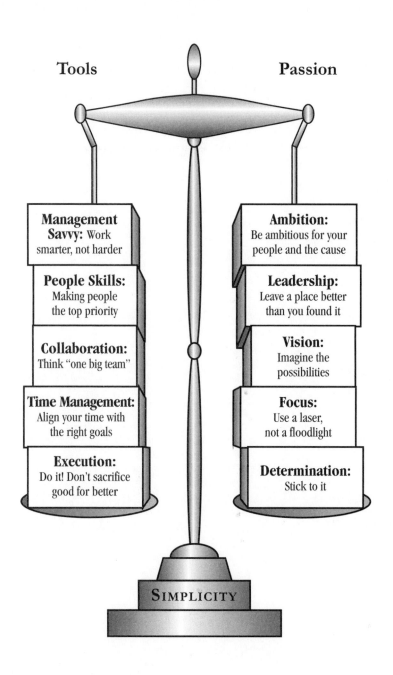

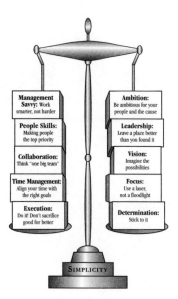

Introduction

In the summer of 2005, Tom Schmitt gathered his FedEx Solutions division of 500 plus employees at a town hall meeting to set the direction for the coming business year. But he wanted to share more than just a business plan with his colleagues. Over the past five years, his Solutions division had grown from a 40-person rogue SWAT team into a powerful force helping generate sales across the entire spectrum of the FedEx portfolio. That achievement had not been preordained. Tom and his team could have made mistakes along the way that would have prevented the division's phenomenal growth. It had been a tremendous learning experience for both Tom and the team, and he wanted to share some of the things he had learned about leadership, teamwork, and the excitement that grows out of satisfying and useful work.

As he thought about the remarks he would make, Tom realized he and the team had made effective use of many *tools,* including management, people skills, collaboration, and execution. But those tools alone hadn't gotten the job done. To grow so rapidly and become such a valuable component of FedEx's overall business also had required *passion*. Ambition, vision, and leadership were among the passions that had propelled Tom and other leaders to success. The model that emerged from Tom's thinking drew on the descriptions psychologists and others who study the brain had devised years ago: the left side of the brain controls logic and analysis, and the right side controls creativity and imagination. Leadership, Tom realized, is a balance between the two. But that wasn't all. Underlying good management was the concept of simplicity. Sure, business in a fast-changing and highly competitive world could look enormously complex. But even the most complex problems could be broken down into simple components and then solved. The key to leadership success, Tom determined, was to build a foundation centered on simplicity and then employ the right combination of tools and passions to accomplish great things. He depicted his "leadership scale" on a simple laminated card that he would hand out to everyone in the meeting.

While Tom was busily growing his Solutions group at FedEx, across town Attorney Arnold Perl was honing his own leadership skills in another pressure cooker environment. The stakes were high. For decades Memphians had tried to coax a national sports team to relocate to their city. Securing a major league sports franchise was the key to making that Mississippi River city the major player it had long dreamed of becoming. Now the realization of that dream was in Arnold's hands. The prize was closer than it had ever been before. The Grizzlies, a Vancouver NBA team, was ready to head south. Only one hurdle remained: the team wanted a new arena, and they wanted to see basketballs bouncing on that new floor within three years. As chairman of the newly formed New Memphis Arena Public Building Authority (PBA), Arnold had three years and a $250-million budget with which to deliver a state-of-the-art, multipurpose sports and entertainment facility. Miss the deadline and the team could—and probably would—exercise its escape clause and leave Memphis with an empty dream.

To get the commitment of the various PBA members, Arnold decided to hold a retreat aimed at creating a mission statement and guiding principles for the huge project. What emerged from several days of discussion and debate was a small laminated red card, about the size of a typical credit card. That little red card became the PBA's mantra. It captured in just a few words all the information contained in multiple complex agreements, including the mammoth project and operating accords written by lawyers. The mission statement was simply "Build It Right." It was followed by seven guiding principles, including "On Time and Within Budget." The red card was more than a list of aspirations. It not only envisioned results, but it also expressed the commitment to those results in a simple, straightforward way for a disbelieving public. The red card created a "checklist" to go by and the "scorecard" on which to be judged. Arnold kept his team focused, and the doors to the FedExForum opened before the deadline and within budget, an almost unheard of accomplishment in the world of massive civic projects.

Tom and Arnold came up with their concepts of simplicity, tools, and passions independently of one another. Had they not met, it is very likely that they each would have gone on using the concepts to achieve great things in their own careers. In talking, Arnold and Tom were able to validate the usefulness of their shared approach. If they had not met, it is doubtful whether either of them would have put them to paper so that others could benefit from them. By sheer coincidence Tom, in his position at FedEx, and Arnold, in his position as a management attorney and community leader in Memphis, began discussing their management philosophies at civic meetings and other forums around Memphis. Only then did it dawn on them that each independently had come to the same simple solutions. The result is this book.

KEEPING IT SIMPLE

This book tells you how to apply simple solutions to complex challenges and become an excellent leader in the process. The book is filled with practical ideas, case studies, real-world examples and anecdotes from the authors' experiences, in the private and public sectors. There are tips and tools you can try immediately. Most important, though, is the underlying philosophy of leadership as something (a) that can be learned; (b) that is a practical, powerful way of building relationships; and (c) that gets results.

Neither the tools and the passions, nor the left-brain, right-brain dichotomy of logic and intuition are new. As managers we've all been trained to use certain management tools. We also know that people with a passion for what they do bring more contagious energy and imagination to a subject than those who aren't passionate. What is new in this book is the methodology of effectively combining skills and passions on a foundation of simplicity. Using our approach, we feel that any manager can discover ways to change the context of a job and open new paths to intellectual excitement, innovation, and career advancement.

We believe that simplicity is the fundamental foundation for management. It is such an important concept in leadership that we devote the first chapter to that subject alone. Amid all the complexity of modern business, it is sometimes tough not to get bogged down in details and complexity. We admire leaders who can "boil things down to their essence"—who can provide focus by bringing complex problems down to a simple problem statement. This book will teach you this core management technique.

That same philosophy of simplicity pervades the entire book. The remaining chapters each deal with a key attribute. Each of the five tools—practical, left-brain approaches to leadership—is matched to a corresponding "passion"—the creative right-brain approaches that provide us with imagination and insight. More important, as you work through the book you'll find that all of the tools and passions also are related to one another. That interrelationship is where the real power of *Simple Solutions* becomes evident.

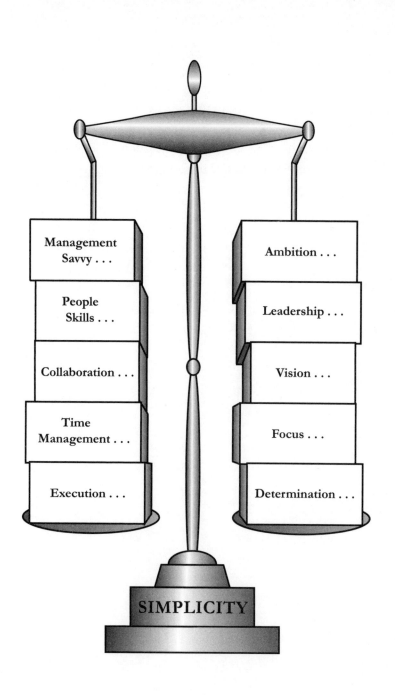

CHAPTER 1

Simplicity: The Foundation of Leadership

*Plain question and plain answer make the shortest
road out of most perplexities.*

—Mark Twain

As a manager, you live in a complex, fast-moving
world. Every day you set goals, assign tasks to employees, formulate budgets, and prepare reports and
reviews. You look for ways to cut costs. You hire, fire,
promote, or transfer your staff members. You attend
to your customers who need service. New competitors arise; they develop new products and services.
All the while the economy and the business environment keep changing at an increasingly rapid pace,
and technology seems to redefine itself overnight.
Tons of information comes at you at lightening speed,
making it increasingly difficult to make decisions.
Complexity increases exponentially. Getting anything
done often seems impossible.

One of the ways great business leaders differentiate themselves is by cutting through all that "noise" and boiling things down to a simple statement, vision, or direction. It isn't easy. To find an all-encompassing, easy-to-understand statement requires clarity of thought and brings into play the balance between the right brain and the left. It starts with rigorous logic in the left side of the brain and then draws on intuition from the right side to weed out extraneous thoughts and keep crucial ideas. Most of us have often thought: "If I had had more time, I would have written a shorter letter."

"Google" the classic quote on page 15 and you'll see it attributed to everyone from Mark Twain to Einstein. Blaise Pascal actually said it first. But it doesn't matter who said it. That simple statement in itself captures one of the key characteristics of simplicity—achieving it isn't simple. It actually takes longer to write a short, concise, "to-the-point" letter than it takes to get all your points across in a rambling, unfocused monologue. Similarly, it's more difficult to formulate a concise and convincing vision and strategy for a business or public venture than to prepare a 100-page report that explains every issue implication. Simple is powerful because it keeps us focused and on track; it's easy to communicate and it's easy to measure. That's why Tom and Arnold both base their leadership philosophy on simplicity.

THE PURPLE PROMISE

Ask any FedEx employee what his or her job is, and the response is likely to be an instant recitation of The Purple Promise: "I will make every FedEx experience outstanding." The details may differ depending on whether you're talking to a pilot, a courier, or a sorting facility manager, but the simple objective is universally understood by FedEx employees anywhere in the world. It is an example of boiling performance down to its essence and giving everyone the ability to focus on what is important. But make no mistake: behind that simplicity are incredibly complex systems and processes that underlie the thousands of planes, trucks, and packages making their way to their individual destinations.

Think about the complexity of your own situation as a manager. You have goals that have to be achieved, people you need to lead, job descriptions to write, processes to put in place, systems to monitor, and deadlines to meet. But what are the common denominators within all this complexity? What is the key focus area for you and your team? What is the essence of your job? Try to formulate this into a simple statement that applies to everyone on your team. Then start communicating that simple statement to everyone in the organization, from your boss right down to your newest hire. You will be surprised how focused people will become, how willing to work hard on what matters, and how willing they will be to weed out what does not contribute to their team's key focus.

Once you simplify your own job, you need to become an evangelist for simplification among your employees. When a team member comes to you with a long story about how her project is in jeopardy because people are not cooperating with her and "that's what's causing this problem here and that problem there," stop her. Tell her you're interested in her problem and want to help, but you both need to get to the real problem. Encourage her to go back to her office and take the time to distill the issue to a simple statement with no more than three main bullet points. That clarity of thought will help both of you focus your efforts on finding a productive solution, rather than flailing away at the complexity of it all.

As a manager you aren't flying solo. Your job is to get other people to do the things they need to do to help your company reach its goals. Thus, it's important for you to be able to communicate to your team as to what they're supposed to be doing, and how and why they're supposed to be doing it. This is where simplicity really begins to pay dividends. If you have clarity of thinking and can reduce your business goals and problems into simple, easy-to-understand statements, your ability to communicate will be much more powerful than someone whose ideas get lost in the details. We've all heard the wondrous clarity that disguised deep complexity when President John F. Kennedy, in his inaugural speech, urged Americans to, "Ask not what your country can do for you—ask what you can do for your country."

When you think about it, the path to leadership really is simple: clarity of thought leads to simplicity, which leads to focus and powerful communication and that's the essence of leadership. Procter and Gamble, one of the world's most successful companies in the competitive field of consumer products, understands the power of simplicity. It's in a tough business, one in which customers in different parts of the globe have different tastes. To make it more complicated, all those different customers' tastes are changing all the time. Procter and Gamble's products have to perform, so it is a given that the chemistry and technology behind them have to be right. But they also have to be marketable, with the right packaging and marketing and at the right price to sell in volume while returning a profit. That's a pretty complex challenge. Yet every single proposal, every internal idea at Procter & Gamble, is distilled into a one-page memo. That's the only way it makes the rounds. That's about as simple as you can imagine and stands in sharp contrast to the typical company that produces a 200-page business case with an appendix as a starting point of a conversation.

McKinsey & Company, one of the most respected consulting firms in the world, has a different, although equally powerful, approach to simplicity. At McKinsey you hear over and over again that good things come in threes. There aren't *10* root causes for a problem or *five* ways to improve performance. *Three* is the magic number. McKinsey's "threes" approach to simplicity puts a strong emphasis on getting down to the essentials, the three critical things that matter.

FOCUSING THE CHAMBER OF COMMERCE

Both Tom and Arnold serve on the Memphis Regional Chamber of Commerce. Anyone who is familiar with chambers of commerce knows that they are engaged in a myriad of activities. The Memphis Chamber was no different and both Tom and Arnold could see that this Chamber lacked a focus. Ask 20 different people what the Chamber was all about and you'd get 20 different answers. There was a reason for that. With the best of intentions, Chamber executives and board members took on many causes, ranging from federal legislation support to local zoning issues, from minimum wage debates to park access roads. There was nothing simple about their agenda. But the result of spreading themselves too thin was this: while the Chamber was involved in many things, it was ineffective in most.

Memphis Regional Chamber

Mission:
To firmly establish the Memphis region as a dynamic, growing, energetic metropolitan region strongly connected the global marketplace.

1. Economic Development
Aggressively promote Business Retention and Expansion by attracting 8,000 new jobs and meet or exceed $1 Billion in new private sector capital investments

★ *Create 8,000 new jobs. (Metro Strategy)*

★ *Reach or exceed $1 Billion new private sector development within the Memphis MSA. (Metro Strategy)*

★ *Reach $300 Million in new capital investments and 2,000 jobs from the bioscience sector as a target within the overall jobs and capital investment goals. (Metro Strategy)*

★ *Complete a minimum of 400 Existing Business calls. (Metro Strategy)*

★ *Increase site visits from 100 to 140 by prospective business clients. (Metro Strategy)*

★ *Initiate Corporate Relocation Program enlisting local CEOs and business representatives for targeted calls. (Metro Strategy)*

★ *Draft multi-year business plan for "Think Memphis Fund" determining new annual budget, recognizing a minimum need of $2.6 Million annually. (Increase of $1.4 Million)*

★ *Increase resources to implement strategies through the following Councils:*
- *BioWorks* $100,000   (Metro)
- *Regional Logistics* $200,000   (Metro & Regional)
- *Regional Econmic Dev.* $ 50,000   (Regional)
These funds are a portion of the $1.4 Million desired increase in the Think Memphis Fund.

Think MEMPHIS
www.memphischamber.com

2. Community Building
Enhance the Memphis Region's marketability by developing amenities, image and leadership within the region.

★ *Determine feasibility of Image Building Campaign. Conduct focus groups and present recommendation by June 2005. (Talent)*

★ *Complete talent recruitment and retention assessment. Plan and determine implementation strategy by March 2005. (Talent)*

★ *Determine feasibility and identify partners for "Committee for a Better Memphis" by November 2005. (Metro)*

★ *Complete $6 Million Building Memphis Campaign and occupy space by December 1, 2005.*

Purpose:
To serve our members and partners by improving the quality of life through regional economic prosperity.

Memphis Regional Chamber
22 North Front Street | Suite 200
Memphis, Tennessee 38103
901.543.3500 | 901.543.3510 (fax)
www.memphischamber.com

To work effectively and to get its message across the Chamber needed focus. Using the same approach they had used in other complex projects, Tom and Arnold put their heads together to find the organization's core objectives. The result: economic development and community building emerged as the Chamber's raison d'etre. From those two core objectives, Tom and Arnold were able to distill 10 key initiatives that supported the two objectives. To ensure that everyone in Memphis understood these objectives and initiatives, the Chamber produced laminated cards—one side showed at the top the economic development objective and the core initiatives and goals that supported that objective, and the other side showed the community-building objective and the key initiatives behind this. Today, whenever a new idea or initiative is brought to the Chamber, someone is likely to pull out the card to see if the suggestion has a place on it. Thus the card focuses everyone—the board, Chamber leadership, and even the media and public—on the Chamber's core mission.

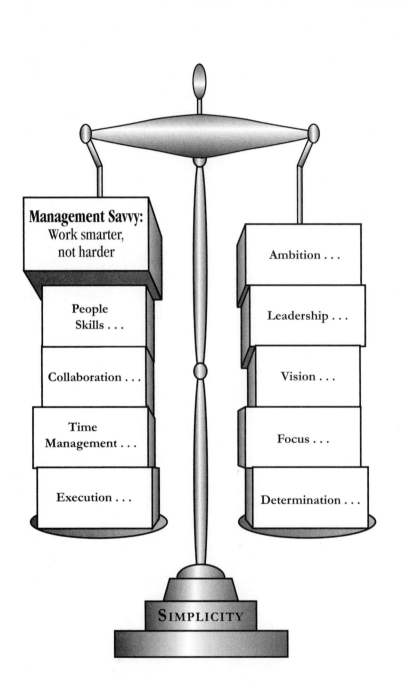

CHAPTER **2**

Management Savvy: Work Smarter, Not Harder

Efficiency is concerned with doing things right.
Effectiveness is doing the right things.

—Peter F. Drucker

You didn't start your career as a middle manager. If you're like most middle managers in most companies, you started your career in a functional specialty. It may have been operations, marketing, finance, or human resources. In a few companies, it could have been in some much more esoteric area. Plenty of middle managers (as well as CEOs) in pharmaceutical companies started as scientists, many airline executives started as pilots, and many utility executives started their careers climbing telephone poles. Where you started doesn't matter. The point is, now you're a manager, not an accountant or an engineer or a scientist. The skills you employed in any one of those functional specialties are probably useful to you today and always will be. But as a manager you're going to be developing and using a whole new set of skills, the most important of which are the subject of this book.

Managing is the art and science of *getting other people to do the things that need to be done.* It certainly sounds simple enough: Just tell someone to do something. But it isn't nearly that easy. You've probably felt the frustration at one time or another when you asked your boss why you've been given a certain task that didn't make sense to you. "Because I said so," is your manager's answer. Infuriating, isn't it? Now that you're in a position to be asked why you're assigning your direct reports to certain tasks, you've got to give them answers that really count. To do that, you need to understand your job in many contexts.

"WHAT WOULD HAVE TO BE TRUE?"

In an ocean of middle managers, how can you stand out as someone who has a savvy take on business? It's simple. Ask and answer some key questions that will question the status quo and make a difference in your company. The idea is to overcome incrementalism, the deadly enemy of innovation. Too many middle managers are trapped by incrementalism—taking problems or issues and setting a goal of making them better a little bit at a time. They're given incremental goals from their management that set targets for a 3 percent gain in this or a 5 percent increase in that, and they usually execute them well and hit the targets. In other words, they're good managers. But in their obsession with devising plans and allocating resources and manpower to hit those targets, they lose sight of the possibility of making a quantum leap. They never take the time to set and reach an amazing goal because they are too focused on reaching an incremental goal. You can ask those questions in all sorts of ways, but we've found that a useful form is to ask, "What would have to be true. . . . ?" Fill in the blank with whatever quantum goal you want to reach, then answer the question.

In Tom's division, one area is charged with calculating and administering variable incentive compensation for the sales force. This bonus pay varies depending on how well a sales professional does in reaching revenue and other business targets and is calculated according to complex formulas that change as business conditions change. Every year, more than 50 people spend long hours working nights and on weekends to make the myriad adjustments in the compensation formulas. These adjustment requests result each quarter in the fair award of bonus money based on several approved "special circumstances" type rules. Interpreting these rules is a process rife with complexity and uncertainty. In the past, this department has had more than 3,000 requests for adjustments each quarter, sometimes continuing well after the quarter had ended. Sales professionals had no clue during the quarter what their efforts, whether good or poor, would yield in bonus pay because the formulas for adjusting out-of-the-ordinary changes to their territories or customers' circumstances were not constant. Not exactly the best way to motivate someone to work harder.

When this department was moved into Tom's division, his management philosophy began to change how these adjustments were viewed. Had he been a typical incremental manager, he would have demanded that his team begin calculating how to reduce the number of adjustments each quarter by 5 percent. Assuming his team met the objective, the result would have been a reduction in the number of adjustments by a whopping 150. That sounds like a drop in the bucket, but it would definitely be progress. And by the end of the year there would be 600 fewer adjustments. Sounds great, doesn't it? Sure, until you consider that there would still be 2,400 adjustments each quarter, and you'd still have a frustrated sales force that wouldn't be able to predict how much bonus they might earn.

Instead, Tom posed this question to his management team: "What would have to be true to get rid of *all* the adjustments?" Now there was a challenge and one worth tackling. The answer didn't get them to zero, but over the course of just two quarters it did get them to 1,000 adjustments and more improvement lies ahead. The way to get to breakthrough achievements (that go far beyond incremental improvements) is all in the approach. Asking "what would have to be true for there to be zero adjustments" results in a different approach than just asking for a 5 percent improvement. The team ended up challenging, simplifying, and eliminating entire business rules. That quantum approach also changed the interaction with sales management. Expecting sales management to submit "zero" requests for adjustments sets a very different mindset and tone.

Because Tom sticks to his philosophy, his team focuses on the amazing goal, not the incremental goal. The people Tom chooses to work closely with him learn to ask the right questions, the ones that pose real challenges, not incremental challenges. That's what makes you think differently. It's how managers make breakthroughs, and it's what makes them stand out. It's what makes them leaders.

CONTENT TRUMPS PROCESS

Asking breakthrough questions to achieve breakthrough results is one important ingredient of being a savvy manager. Another is communicating effectively. Simply put, you should always communicate about *content,* not *process.* For example, think for a moment

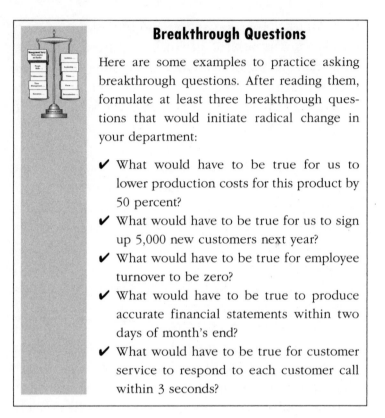

Breakthrough Questions

Here are some examples to practice asking breakthrough questions. After reading them, formulate at least three breakthrough questions that would initiate radical change in your department:

✔ What would have to be true for us to lower production costs for this product by 50 percent?

✔ What would have to be true for us to sign up 5,000 new customers next year?

✔ What would have to be true for employee turnover to be zero?

✔ What would have to be true to produce accurate financial statements within two days of month's end?

✔ What would have to be true for customer service to respond to each customer call within 3 seconds?

about where you are in terms of a specific project in your division. If you check in with a team member about progress on a project and he starts telling you about the next management review date or team "check-in" meeting, you're getting a process answer, not a content answer. In other words, he's not telling you how the project is going; he's telling you how the project approval and check-in process is coming along. That isn't surprising. It's the typical response.

But it doesn't give you any real information. It doesn't give you information that you might need later when your own manager asks you how your team's initiatives are faring. Unless you consider "Oh, we're doing a progress review in two weeks" a proper update for *your* manager.

Here's how content-driven communication works: if you ask a question and your team member knows you want a *content* answer, you may get something like this: "We think it will be a go if we can price aggressively and increase the capacity utilization of the warehouse from 40 to 80 percent—we'll know the answer on that in time for the review two weeks from now."

Now that's news you can use! Armed with that information, you might be able to contribute an idea or two about how to help out. In any case, you now have a solid answer to give your manager, who himself may have an idea about how to get there. Thinking in terms of content, not process, is how business savvy helps you help the company make money.

Putting content over process is useful in other ways, too. Think about all the meetings you attend. It's very likely you consider many of them prime sources of wasted time and frustration. Many meetings are ceremonial events, held simply because that's what we do at 9 A.M. Monday or 2 P.M. Wednesday. They're about process, not content. If you can turn your team meetings into occasions for discussions of content rather than process, everyone will emerge from them with a better knowledge of how to do his or her job more efficiently and effectively with a better chance of achieving a breakthrough.

Process over Content: Case Study

At ABC Company, managers frequently are asked to make brief presentations at their vice presidents' staff meetings. It's often a stressful situation, since the audience includes one's own manager and possibly a director or vice president or two, as well. Joe was new to management and the company when he got his first summons to "update" his vice president on a key initiative owned by Joe's team. The project, which carries a budget of more than $1 million, was an internal online knowledge management system that would allow anyone in the company to access research, presentations, case studies, budgets, and proprietary data by product lines, customer segments, and geographic markets.

Joe was confident and even looking forward to the presentation. He knew the material—after all it was his team's most important work and he'd been on top of things, making sure his project team stayed focused and busy. He'd also heard enough about his predecessor to know that in the past, loose ends had tended to go unnoticed and project updates were often haphazard and incomplete.

Not going to happen on my watch, Joe told his team.

He met with each member of the team, gathering details and timelines. He was determined to arm himself with everything his vice president could possibly want to know. He knew the condition the project was in when he moved in as manager, and he knew how many long hours he and his team had worked to get things on track and get back in synch with the project timeline. The databases that were so crucial to the project's success were up to date. All navigation bars for the tool had been loaded for testing. Budget numbers were documented and showed the project clearly within the boundaries. Several employees who were often late and had frequent absenteeism had been talked to and coached and were showing up on time every day for work. These employees—in fact, all of his employees—appeared, on the surface at least, to be enthusiastic and excited about the project and proud of their involvement. All the signs pointed to success for Joe's

MANAGEMENT SAVVY: WORK SMARTER, NOT HARDER

management skills, and he anticipated basking in the glow of approval when his vice president got a first hand view of how he'd pulled it all together.

On the day of the presentation, Joe arrived early in spite of the late night he'd had proofing the presentation until the words swam before his eyes. It would be perfect. His own manager, not one to interfere at the manager level, would be seeing it for the first time too, and Joe looked forward to letting his own boss know how the loose ends were now in place and how much better shape things were in since Joe took over.

The moment arrived and Joe moved to center stage in the conference room. There were a few more people than Joe had expected, but he'd had extra copies made and again, Joe congratulated himself on his foresight. This is it, he thought. Here I am in front of the woman who can make or break my career. This is my day.

Joe began his moment in the sun by talking about just how bad things were when he took over. He detailed the database updates, the testing schedules for the newly designed navigation bars. He showed budget slides and workflows. One slide showed a drop in absenteeism on Joe's team and another showed hours spent on various levels of the project. His presentation was flawless and he built a clear picture of how he made things right. It was a clear win.

Or, so he thought.

Joe got his first indication things might not be as flawless as he'd imagined when he noticed his manager seemed to be a little jumpy. Then, a couple of slides later, Joe's heart sank as he noticed his vice president actually reading something on her hand-held. He recovered somewhat when she again began paying attention and when he finished his final slide and no one had questions, Joe regained his earlier sense of well-being. "No questions!" he told his team later. "I covered everything they could have possibly wanted."

Or did he?

What did Joe tell his vice president?

- ✔ How bad things were when he took over. (Did Joe's director know he was going let the vice president in on this?)
- ✔ How well he and his team had "stuck to the timelines." (Timelines are beneficial, but not when they're only about things that have already occurred.)
- ✔ The budget summary for the past month. (Unless the budget is significantly over or under, this is not an issue for this meeting.)
- ✔ Too many tactical issues were included for this type meeting:

37

—How well the databases were maintained. (Upper management assumes these things are being done unless they've heard otherwise.)

—How quickly and efficiently testing is going for the new navigation bars.

—How smoothly the past three system loads had been.

—How previous employee problems with absenteeism had been dealt with.

—How many hours each member of his team had spent devoted to this vital project.

—The date of the next project update.

Joe's vice president attends staff meetings led by the company's top management where decisions are made that affect the company far into the future. Prioritization of company resources is debated and resolved. In other words, it's the meeting where the rubber meets the road and a project can live or die by the outcome. It's also the meeting where collaboration at the highest levels begins. Vice presidents can offer the support of their own teams.

Is Joe's vice president armed with the right information to push his project forward? Can she ask for help or needed advice from the top leadership of her company?

No.

The only information she could pass along is that Joe's employees are working every day and sticking to their timelines. Databases are being updated and project updates are being given. Is this what your CEO wants to know about a project that's costing more than $1 million? If your CEO is typical, he probably assumes the people his company employs show up for work—and if they don't, he has levels of management in place to deal with those kinds of problems and with tactical issues such as database updates and timelines. What the CEO doesn't know (yet) is how soon he'll be able to see the impact from Project XYZ.

Here are some things Joe should have covered:

✔ What are the most important elements of the databases (for example, the case studies) and what impact will their availability online have on sales people's revenue generation?

✔ How will this knowledge management system set ABC Company apart from the competition?

BREAKTHROUGH THINKING IN THE PUBLIC SECTOR

Asking "What would need to be true" is just as important in the public sector, where incrementalism is just as prevalent and often stands in the way of breakthroughs. Arnold, chairman of the Memphis-Shelby

County Airport Authority, saw the power of break-through thinking when FedEx, by far the Memphis Airport's biggest customer and a major source of jobs and tax revenue for the city, was growing rapidly. It needed more space at the airport for hangars, ramps, and sorting facilities. But it was landlocked with nowhere to expand because the Tennessee Air National Guard's facility for its C-17 cargo jets was based on an adjacent 103-acre parcel that it wasn't about to abandon. It looked like a stalemate that would force FedEx to look for expansion at airports in other cities.

Then the Air Force changed the Tennessee Air National Guard's mission, a change that would require the guard to switch to much larger C-5 cargo jets. As a result of the change, the guard was going to have to spend $125 million to upgrade the Memphis facility. Then the Airport Authority staff came up with a "win win" solution for both the Air Guard and FedEx Express. The Air Guard conversion project was not ideal because the existing base did not have sufficient space to accommodate all of the large C-5 aircraft and provide the necessary force protection required by all military bases since the events of September 11, 2001. FedEx Express needed more space to add capacity. It seems like a simple idea—take the $125 million in Air Guard funds and build a new base on a greenfield site on the opposite side of the airport that would be out of the way of FedEx Express. After the new base was completed, the Air Guard would return the old base to the Airport Authority who then would lease the base to FedEx Express.

Both parties liked the idea from the start, but there were problems. The $125 million was enough money to modify the existing base, but fell nearly $100 million short of what it would cost to build a new base at a green field site. The problem was solved when FedEx Express agreed to provide the difference in the cost. That amount of money would be used as prepayment of rent for the old base for a period of 30 to 50 years. Negotiations over financial terms between FedEx Express and the Air Guard took place over many months. At one point, it appeared that the negotiations had failed, but during a meeting on a different subject between Arnold and senior executives of FedEx Express the negotiations were revived and later successfully completed. To speed the construction of the new base, the Airport Authority agreed to be contracting agent and manager for the $220 million project. Clearly this was the out-of-the-box breakthrough thinking that made a difference to the airport and the community at large.

As a manager, it is easy to get bogged down in competing interests: marketing may want more funding for advertising campaigns, sales wants to hire more reps and finance wants everyone to cut costs. It is tempting to narrowly focus on limited resources (for example, the specific parcel of land in the airport example)—then fight it out between different constituents (for example, Air National Guard versus FedEx). Breakthrough thinking cuts through these turf wars by asking radical questions: How can we all get what we need? What would need to be true for us to double margins? What would need to be true for both the Guard and FedEx to have sufficient space at the airport? How can we find the resources/funds for this?

HOW BUSINESS SAVVY ARE YOU?

If you've been doing all those things recommended earlier in the chapter for a few weeks or more, the following business savvy quiz will give you some idea about how well you're doing. If you're just reading the chapter for the first time, it will give you ideas about things to look for as you do your research:

✔ How does your company rank in size within its industry? "Size" can mean many things, but your foray into finance will suggest that some things matter much more than others: revenues, rate of revenue growth, profits, and return on investment. Has your company's ranking in any of those important categories changed significantly for better or worse in the past five years? What is the reason for that?

✔ How does your company compete in its market or markets? Is it the cheapest? The best? The most innovative?

✔ What is your company's competitive advantage? Costs? Geography? Proprietary technology? How durable is that advantage? Could a new competitor suddenly spring up with a new technology? Could a competitor suddenly spring up in another country?

✔ Competitive advantage aside for a moment, what is the economy doing and what is the likely impact on your company?

✔ Who are your customers within the company? Are you effectively delivering what those customers want? Is your customer satisfaction high? Is your price right? Are you delivering value? What do you need to do to increase that value? How are you measuring your customer's satisfaction? Do you know what your customer will need from you two months from now? A year from now? How do you find out?

✔ Who are your suppliers within the company? How is your supplier doing? Are you getting excellent value? Could it be better? Are you clearly communicating your needs to your supplier? Does your supplier know what you will need two months from now? A year from now?

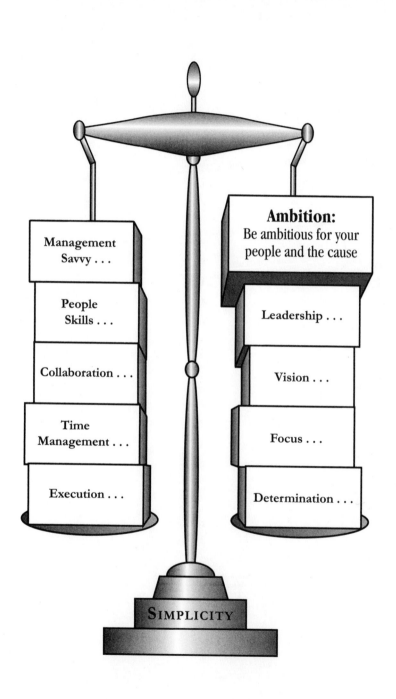

CHAPTER 3

Ambition: Be Ambitious for Your People and the Cause

Everybody is ambitious. The question is whether he is ambitious to be or ambitious to do.

—Jean Monnet

You wouldn't be reading this book if you weren't ambitious. You probably wouldn't be a manager, either. Ambition, defined as "an ardent desire for rank, fame, or power," is most likely what gets you and others with great ambition out of bed and heading for the office each weekday morning. It's a powerful motivating force. But, like any other powerful force, it can be used well and to great benefit or it can be used badly with dire consequences. There is a fine line between "good ambition" and "bad ambition." Good ambition promotes the interests of your colleagues, your company, and, ultimately, yourself. Bad ambition is all about "me, me, me." You spend half your energy thinking up ways to get ahead faster or how to trip someone before they trip you, instead of focusing that energy on something productive. As subtle as you try to be, your motives are still obvious to colleagues, and you earn the reputation you deserve.

There are some good reasons why focusing on ambition or on yourself doesn't work:

If all your focus is on "working your way up" you have less energy and mindshare left for focusing on the business, finding new creative solutions to problems, and making a difference. Ultimately, the energy you spend on polishing your career is wasted. If you can redirect that energy toward finding ways to make a difference to your team, your colleagues, and your customers, your ambition will fulfill itself automatically.

Focusing on getting ahead creates a perception problem. You may be a great manager and highly effective at what you do, but your ambition creates a perception that you're "in it only for yourself." As a result your relationships lack the crucial element of trust, a key ingredient in successful executive teams.

MAKING THE "B" TEAM

Tom knows from firsthand experience how "bad" ambition can set you on the wrong track. McKinsey & Company is one of the world's premier consulting firms, and only smart, ambitious people are hired as consultants. Tom joined McKinsey straight out of college in Germany, where the company operates a little differently than it does in the United States. In Germany, Tom and others like him earn "credit" toward their advancement with McKinsey before leaving temporarily to get an advanced business degree. In the United States, however, McKinsey consultants earn this "credit" only *after* they have earned their MBA. After a year with McKinsey in Germany, Tom went to Harvard for his MBA, and then rejoined McKinsey in the United States.

Imbued with the notion that his experience in Germany had earned him some credit, Tom simply assumed he would become a project manager before any of his colleagues who were hired at the same time. He didn't try to hide this ambition. It defined him as someone eager to "get ahead." And, sure enough, he got ahead. He was the first in his group to become a project manager. But before long, Tom noticed that the customers he really wanted were going to other teams. Coworkers he sought as collaborators on projects were being assigned to other project managers.

Only after a while did it dawn on Tom that those customers and preferred teammates were actually being assigned to project managers who didn't "dive right in" as did Tom. Instead, they took a more measured approach to their career advancement. Sure, Tom got there first. He went up a level before his colleagues did, but he didn't like what he saw. It wasn't long before he realized he wasn't getting the best assignments and, to make matters worse, the work he was doing definitely wasn't going to get him the visibility he needed for the partnership track at McKinsey.

It was a defining experience for Tom. "It was completely counterproductive," he recalls today. "I spent too much time trying to get ahead and wound up in the wrong place." He resolved to run his life differently after that, seeking the challenges and opportunities that "felt right," rather than simply seeking promotions and power. In 1998, the headhunters discovered Tom and he wound up with competing offers. One was from General Electric Capital Corporation, the most powerful division of one of the world's most respected companies. With historic roots back to Thomas Alva Edison, this company's long-standing reputation for performance excellence made it an attractive draw.

The other offer was from FedEx. Like GE, it was a very successful company. It got high marks for entrepreneurial energy, wonderful customer service, and had a reputation as a great place to work. But it was definitely a small company and a relative newcomer compared to GE. On the surface, it was a no-brainer. Who wouldn't want to go to work for the most prestigious division of a prominent company like GE, with its soaring stock price and its perfect location in Fairfield, Connecticut, a beautiful town close to the cultural riches of New York City? Tom and his wife, Petra, both trained academically and professionally to carefully analyze details, dutifully prepared spreadsheets comparing the offers. No surprise there. GE came out on top every time when compared statistically to FedEx. Yet an "indefinable something" spoke to Tom, and in the end he chose FedEx. Why? Because it "felt right." Tom had learned through his previous experiences to listen to his intuition, despite the fact that the numbers stacked up in favor of GE. Needless to say, it was the right choice.

Today, Tom judges his success using a different yardstick. He no longer looks at how fast he's rising up the corporate ladder, although he's making a steady climb at FedEx. Instead, Tom prefers to look at a typical week and weigh the good days against the bad. Is he happy and excited about his job four out of five days? Unlike his McKinsey days, Tom now considers not only his career but also the future of his team, which now numbers more than 1,000.

"Am I making a serious attempt to find ways to help the people who work with me to be excited four days out of five?" Tom asks. "I hope so. For me, that's what channels professional ambition into what it should be: creating winners instead of counting the months until you get your next promotion."

THE INGREDIENTS OF GOOD AMBITION

Where can you have the most impact? The ambition that drives you is yours to shape for better or worse. More often than not, the person who strives to make a positive impact on other people and who doesn't spend too much time worrying about getting ahead is the one who will wake up one day to realize that somehow he has "gotten ahead." Better yet, he's not just moving toward a leadership role, he's enjoying a sense of satisfaction, a feeling that often eludes those who seek only self-promotion.

It isn't that the higher levels you want to reach are simply going to fall into your lap. Obviously, you're going to need to have a vision for what you'd like to achieve for yourself, and do periodic due diligence to see how you're tracking and to make adjustments as needed. But if you're focused on doing the right things, like delivering high-quality, on-time output with a team that you motivate to perform at full speed, you'll be surprised how much you'll be noticed by the right people.

You can see the results of making that positive impact on people in friends and colleagues who volunteer in the community, perhaps as Boy Scout leaders or as coaches for the community soccer league. They aren't "getting ahead" in terms of power, pay, or promotion, but they feel good about themselves and the impact they're having on the kids who look to them for guidance. Your challenge as a manager is to conduct yourself in such a way that you capture that same feeling of contribution and satisfaction on the job.

The key to harnessing your ambition is to concentrate on making a difference that leaves a project or a person better than before. When you take on a new project, a new team or new responsibilities, remember that with that responsibility comes the opportunity to create and mold whatever it is you're doing to make it better. It is yours to shape. It pays to take a step back and figure out what change, impact, or end product you would like to see as a result of your efforts. Once you have that vision firmly in mind, you can channel your energy and your team's energy toward that vision.

CALIBRATING AMBITION

Good ambition rests on that old proverb "Know thyself." Achieving positive ambition is critically dependent on some introspection that results in identifying the "authentic" you, setting your own standards and not letting others set them for you. It requires self-confidence to set your own course, but if you can achieve that goal life becomes easier. You're not working less, but you're enjoying it more because you're no longer hostage to other people's opinions about what constitutes success for you.

There are ways to calibrate your ambition to ensure that you remain firmly in the realm of good ambition and don't succumb to the temptations of bad ambition. One simple measure is the quality of people you hire. Are you hiring direct reports who are better than you? That might sound like a scary proposition, but really great managers are always on the lookout for team members who are strong in areas that they themselves may not be. When Tom builds a team, he's not looking for skills that mirror his own. In fact, his officer team has attributes or skills that are better than his own in some areas, he says. One of them is highly creative, another is analytical, and the third is skilled at building relationships. The point is, you can't be an expert on everything. There aren't enough hours in the day. But you don't have to be an expert on everything if you're secure enough to let your direct reports do "the heavy lifting" in their own domain specialties. It demonstrates a level of self-confidence that is good for you, for your company, and for your direct reports. The company gets the benefit of their skills and abilities; you are able to gain additional knowledge from them; and your team gets to hone their skills and abilities without fear of retribution from a boss afraid of being shown up. Imagine the impact of a team whose manager hires only those less competent to ensure that no one challenges his position as the top dog. A leader is only as good as the work his team produces. It might help to remember that if you don't hire the best person for the job, your competitor will.

A second measure of how well you're channeling your ambition comes from how other people think you're doing your job. If you're on the fast track, you're doubtless getting periodic performance evaluations. Take them seriously, not simply as report cards that influence compensation and promotions. Performance reviews, when done correctly, can offer valuable insight to help you gauge whether your ambition is matched by your skills. If your boss is astute, he or she will recognize flaws in your performance. You can acknowledge those perfunctorily and then keep doing the things you were doing before, or you can take them seriously, look for the causes and how they manifest themselves, and then start correcting them. That isn't always easy because it can require a change in fundamental behaviors, but it can be done. The best way is to concentrate on the one or two most serious flaws. Develop a plan for correcting them, implement that plan and then seek frequent feedback on how well you're doing. Your manager is the best source of that feedback, but you can, by sharing your plan with close colleagues or even subordinates, make good use of their candid feedback.

THE POWER OF MENTORS

If you don't already have one, get a mentor. Get the best one you can find. It might be your boss if you have sufficient respect for his or her knowledge and skills, or it could be someone higher in the organization. A good mentor will not only serve as a coach who provides valuable knowledge and insight about the company and yourself, he can also be an invaluable advocate for you within the organization. Rest assured—if you're on a fast track, people above you know it and are talking about you. You want someone on your side who will hear, interpret, and influence the "gossip" about you in a way that will have an impact on your career path.

If you aren't already, be a mentor. You should have one associate, preferably a direct report, who you are mentoring. That goes beyond mere supervision. It means taking time to involve that person in your work, offering "life" lessons as they apply to work, steering that person through the corporate culture in a positive way and being genuinely interested in his or her professional and personal success. If you pick your direct reports carefully (and why shouldn't you?), you'll gain self satisfaction—and maybe renewed recognition—when they do well and get promoted or even hired away.

Tom is convinced that mentoring others is not only the right thing to do—it is also a smart and, most importantly, a mutually enriching thing to do. "I make it a point to meet with my direct reports regularly on development issues, separately from more task-oriented sessions," he says. "It helps the employee grow. That's good for them and good for FedEx. I always feel that both sides take something positive away." In addition, Tom is available to everyone in his division for a one-on-one discussion as and when needed. His team members know to use these thought partner sessions on a selective basis.

When Arnold accepted Diversity Memphis' Humanitarian Award in May 2006, he spoke about the impact his invaluable mentor, Jim McGehee, had on his life. Jim maintained that while not everyone is in a position to give back to his or her community, for those who can and do it is personally fulfilling and highly beneficial to transform our cities into real "communities."

Arnold's law firm, Ford & Harrison LLP, has in place a mentoring program for all newly hired lawyers out of law school to accelerate their development as lawyers. The firm also assigns a mentor to all lateral hires coming into the firm to ensure they meet the firm's expectation that clients always get "The Right Response at the Right Time." The mentors at the firm also expose the attorneys to the opportunities for pro-bono work and to taking an active role in Bar activities and community service.

360 Degree Assessments

Three-hundred-sixty-degree assessments have become a popular management tool in the past few years and are an excellent instrument for calibrating your ambition. These assessments may be developed in-house or by an external provider such as a human resources consulting firm. In either case, they usually consist of a detailed survey that goes beyond assessing your performance on the job. They also examine your leadership style, communication skills, and approach to decision making. The survey is completed by several of your direct reports, peers, and by your boss. Some instruments go further than that and include input from front-line employees and several superior relationships (for example, if you're operating in a matrix organization).

The questionnaire is usually completed online and a computer program then tabulates everyone's input and provides it in a summary report that is anonymous by respondent category. This anonymity feature is one reason that 360s are considered a helpful tool. Since feedback cannot be traced back to individual respondents, it can be more candid than in regular performance reviews. Another benefit is the broad range of respondents. Most of us will get at least some performance feedback from our boss, but how often do we get input from peers and direct reports? If we do, the feedback often feels subjective and one-sided. A 360 instrument provides measurability to those "hard-to-pin-down" soft skills by comparing individual scores against norms or standards that may be defined for your company or more generally.

In terms of calibrating your ambition, utilize a 360 degree assessment to compare the feedback with your own self-perception. Where the two diverge, you would do well to analyze the underlying issue by discussing the feedback with your boss, a mentor, or a coach. The best leaders utilize this feedback as a tool to develop their interpersonal skills.

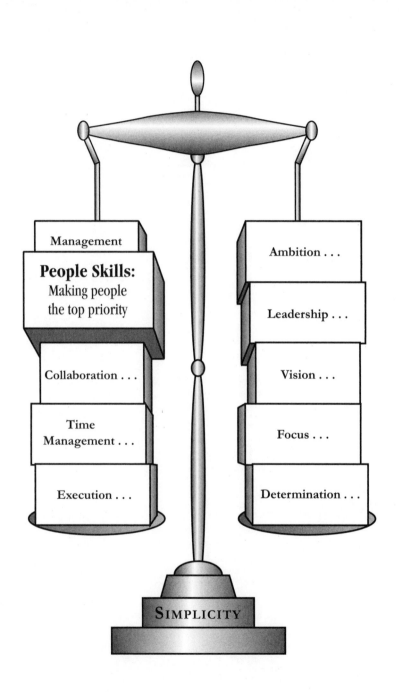

CHAPTER 4

People Skills: Making People the Top Priority

If we take people only as they are, then we make them worse; if we treat them as if they were what they should be, then we bring them to where they can be brought.

—Johann Wolfgang Von Goethe

Resources, full-time employees (FTEs), tools, assets, human resources—call them what you want, they're still the most vital element to a manager's success or failure. Efficient managers can stay on top of tactical issues, and smart managers can think outside the box or come up with innovative solutions. But only a manager destined to be a leader can successfully manage a team of people and instill in them a passion for excellence and meaningful results.

Scott Adams, creator of the Dilbert cartoon phenomenon, has made a name for himself lambasting bad management. He has plenty of material from which to draw. After all, not just anyone can successfully lead people. And among those who do it well, the few who stand out from the rest are those who do the best job of balancing the left brain's analytical tools and right brain's creativity and passion.

"People-Service-Profit" has been the hallmark of management at FedEx since its inception. Simply put, it means people come before service and people come before profit. It's a clear expectation that every employee at every level puts people first, whether those people are customers or colleagues. Imagine investment bankers back in the 1970s getting a pitch from a guy who wanted to start a package delivery service founded on the philosophy that people will come first. Yet that's how FedEx founder Frederick W. Smith started FedEx and he hasn't deviated from that philosophy since. He put people first and they responded in kind. On more than one occasion, FedEx employees have put the company first, whether it was delivering packages from personal vehicles in the early 1970s or spending their own time volunteering to work on the front lines, loading and sorting packages in peak holiday demand times, even after putting in a full day on their regular jobs. FedEx became a global leader in innovation and Smith rose to iconic status with hundreds of thousands of employees who are secure in the knowledge they really do come first.

The "people first" philosophy at FedEx colors the entire atmosphere. Visitors know without being told that people are important. Tom Schmitt saw it and felt it from the start. That's what attracted him to FedEx and helped cement his decision to take a FedEx offer over one being extended by GE Capital, one of the most famous companies in the world. His pros and cons spreadsheet told him one thing, but his heart told him something else. He followed his heart and has never regretted it. What he remembers most about his first visit to FedEx were the amazing people he met. He believes encountering great people who have their hearts in the right places at FedEx is no co-incidence. Instead, it's a byproduct born of more than 30 years of a people first environment.

Making people the priority really is the first step in a cycle of successful employee, successful manager, and successful company. The simple question: "What is the right thing to do for our people?" is the fundamental principle that guides both Tom and Arnold. It isn't always apparent to someone when you're pushing him to stretch and become better that you're doing what's right for that person, but when he attains that goal and realizes that his capabilities have expanded beyond what he thought possible, it all becomes clear.

People skills are among the most important tools a manager can have in his or her "management toolkit," and this chapter explains why people skills are so im-portant and what you can do to improve them. Some of it is philosophical, all about the ways you can develop your own people skills and those of your subordinates to unleash the collective power of collaboration. Another part of it is mechanical: evaluation, hiring, firing, rewards, and communication. But it all boils down to creating positive stimulation and excitement in your job and finding ways to make that stimulation and excitement contagious. When everybody catches it, they and the companies for which they work find themselves in positions to succeed.

Tapping the "discretionary effort" of employees—unleashing that 100 percent or more performance—is what good people skills are all about. As a manager, you have a singular focus: Get people to do the things that need to be done so the company makes money, adding as much value along the way as possible. A motivated employee is more productive, and is both able and willing to put forth that discretionary effort beyond the average or expected performance. The key is to engage employees in a way that makes that discretionary effort the norm.

THE WILL-SKILL MATRIX

Successful management starts with putting the right people in the right job. It sounds easy enough, but in fact it requires some effort to be sure that the person to whom you're assigning a task is the right one for the job. One simple device Tom likes to use is the will-skill matrix that aligns abilities with tasks. One axis is the degree of *will* that the employee exhibits. Think of it as enthusiasm or determination. The other axis is the degree of *skill* that will be required to do the job right. Skills manifest themselves as on-the-job performance, experience, and the training needed for the job at hand. Say a new project will require six employees. Think about them individually, but also in the context of how they all fit on a will-skill matrix. When Tom finds that he has enough team members who bring both the will and the skill to do the job right, he simply gets out of the way and lets the team produce the good results that are almost guaranteed. He can be confident that team members like this, who are highly motivated and skilled in their functional areas, will deliver excellence.

On the other hand, motivation and the best will to get the job done can't overcome a lack of skills necessary to complete a task. Luckily, a motivated employee's desire to learn can make this an easy hurdle to overcome. Options include doing the training yourself, seeking other training sources, or pairing the "high-will/low-skill" employee with one well-seasoned in the required skills. What about the opposite situation when you have an employee who brings the right expertise to the job, but simply isn't motivated to get the job done, the so-called "high-skill/low-will" employee? They can be frustrating and become a management challenge as you seek the right motivation to move this promising employee into the "high-will/high-skill" quadrant of the matrix. Different things motivate different employees. It can be something as broad as the chance to manage others, or something as simple as the promise of getting to deliver a final report to senior management. Your job is to find ways to boost energy around the "will" axis. Even good employees sometimes have trouble getting motivated to make their very best contribution in each and every task, especially if they're doing repetitive work. Fresh roles, even within the context of the same job, are the essence of corporate energy.

Making people your priority means you will never consciously put a team member in a low-will, low-skill role. That's tantamount to putting that person in a position to fail. Sure, it seems like the path of least resistance to simply look for ways to get rid of a low-will, low-skill employee. Matching people to jobs that both motivate them and that match their skill level is not always easy. But if you can solve that problem and get people motivated to use whatever skills they have, those people will become loyal members of the team. People you help succeed not only enjoy greater self-confidence, but they become happier in their jobs.

RECRUIT, DON'T JUST HIRE

Building teams can be easy if you surround yourself with the best people, and that starts with recruiting. The science of recruiting and hiring is really no science at all, but hard work toward establishing criteria, seeking the best candidates, and soliciting input from coworkers to optimize the process. A great example of a successful recruiting process is what transpires at a college football powerhouse. The coach doesn't select the person to fill the quarterback position from among the "walk-ons." The coach knows exactly who he wants, right down to a specific height and weight, a strong arm, the right attitude, leadership ability. Some coaches will scour the country to find the right person. To build your own winning team, you need to do the same thing. You have to know what qualities and skills you need to get the job done right and then go out and find the person with those qualities and skills. Too often, managers aren't willing to make that effort and wind up hiring someone from among the "walk-ons," the applicants who just show up when an opening is announced. They're settling for less than the best and will suffer the consequences.

Even before you talk to the first candidate you have to think long and hard about the skills the job will require. Define the job incorrectly and you will almost automatically hire the wrong person. Once you know the skills that are required, you can begin to match them with a potential employee. But skills alone won't be enough. You also have to look at a person through the lens of personality and attitude. Will this person be willing and able to work as part of a team? Will he or she fit well into your corporate culture?

A critical factor is to recruit for diversity in thought and experience, and never, ever be afraid to hire someone smarter or more accomplished than you. As we said earlier, Tom's three officers in the FedEx Solutions division all have strengths and skills in one area or another that exceed his own. One of the three is more adept than Tom in out-of-the-box creativity, another is a more rigorous and analytic thinker, and the third is a skilled networker. Not only do they bring necessary skills to FedEx, they also stretch Tom's own abilities and skills resulting in continuous improvement for all.

Recruiting is an important part of getting the right people, but it's just the beginning. Managing people well requires a credible system of evaluation applied credibly. Such evaluation processes always have an element of subjectivity, though in good organizations with good performance management tools that subjectivity is minimized as much as possible. Evaluating employees should occur throughout the year; when it is time for formal review, there should be no surprises. Have plenty of time when you do your reviews. By doing them on time, in private, and without interruptions, you will convey the importance of the process.

The evaluation should be a healthy discussion. It should be designed to answer your employee's questions of: "How am I doing? What could I do better?"

The effective manager uses evaluations to improve his own abilities, and he also uses them to raise the level of the people he manages. Nothing is worse than an evaluation system that no one believes in, or a flawed evaluation system that is used to rate and rank people unfairly and with little basis in fact. Nothing is better than one that helps savvy, ambitious employees rise in the organization, or prepares them for better jobs in your or other organizations. Done correctly, these annual or semiannual evaluations offer opportunities and set the stage for conversations about performance that can be difficult to instigate on a day-to-day basis. Summoning an employee for a one-on-one discussion of less than stellar performance is like a trip to the principal's office. The same conversation done in a performance review—where such topics are the norm—is a constructive one. No one likes to tell someone she is a marginal performer or lagging behind others, but you do her no favors by not telling her. You owe your employees a chance to do better and an action plan for improvement that gives the individual another chance to do better, this time armed with information and skills to accomplish the right results. Remember, the emphasis here is on candor, a useful trait to apply in other business interactions. Jack Welch talks about candor being the single most important factor in his success at GE, and he believes that a human resources leader is the second most important person in a company, behind the chairman. Candor is the best kind of communication.

Finally, evaluations are an excellent tool to identify whether a job has clearly defined roles and responsibilities, both for the manager and his employees. If you're struggling in your job, step back and assess whether you really understand your role. What are you supposed to be doing, how does your manager think you should do it and what should the outcomes be? Do the same exercise with your employees. Ask them to assess their own roles and then compare notes. Do you both have the same understanding of roles and responsibilities? If not, now's the time to build alignment.

KNOW YOUR PEOPLE

People skills and leadership are a powerful combination. Successful business relationships and fulfilling personal interaction at home or where we worship each have different dynamics, but fundamentally they are the same. Respect for others, clear communication, striving to achieve consensus, all have their place in each of our social and business environments and always have. When Arnold visited a Sylvania factory in Dyersburg, Tennessee, in 1972, he was surprised to find that unlike the other plants in the lighting products group, it wasn't unionized. When he asked the director of labor relations how the plant had escaped being unionized, he learned that the plant manager had a fundamental rule: each manager was required to talk to each of his employees every day. When the rule was first implemented, the managers tended to put off the conversations until the end of the day. That raised some suspicions among the employees, who thought that the conversations were a tactic to find out how much work had been done that day. The managers started talking to the employees earlier and it had the desired effect. Employees perceived that the managers cared about them as people, evidenced by the fact that the managers learned the names of the employees' spouses and children and shared stories about their weekends. That lesson learned in 1972 is still applicable today and is taught by highly successful managers like Tim Neville at Bridgestone Americas Holding, Inc., who himself in 1972 viewed successful managers as "coaches" and "teachers" who effectively reached out to their teams to get the best results.

Tom is known as one of the more approachable executives as FedEx. Although as his responsibilities grow it's becoming more difficult, Tom still calls everyone working for him on his or her birthday. It's an opportunity to spend a few minutes taking the individual's pulse, how they feel about what they are doing, what resources they may need, or how their families are doing. It's about creating an observation point, a place to stay involved with his team on a personal basis. Tom keeps faithfully to the schedule and has made birthday calls from several continents. He's made calls from Bermuda, Germany, and all points in between. One employee, born on Christmas Eve, wondered aloud one year whether he'd get his call from Tom, who was in Germany with his family. The call came, just as the man's coworkers told him it would. Solutions employees know that whether they are able to answer their telephone or not, no matter what time zone Tom is in or what continent he'll sleep on that night, that birthday call will arrive.

On a more formal basis, every manager in FedEx Services must have among his or her seven or eight annual objectives one item dealing with people development, such as increasing diversity in the promotion pool. Like the other performance objectives, that item has set against it a certain percentage of that year's compensation. Making people skills part of the compensation package ensures that managers don't just give people skills lip service.

TOUGH ON ISSUES, NOT PEOPLE

Companies create good workplaces when they deal with the problems that frustrate the best intentions of employees. One company may hire and fire workers until it gets the results it wants or goes out of business. Another company may step back and understand the root cause of the bad results, fix it, and give its people another chance to succeed. The root of the frustration could be the company's fault, something as simple as inadequate resources or poor training. Or it could be employees who just aren't up to the task. But quickly diagnosing those hurdles and overcoming them is key. FedEx is tough on issues, not on people. That doesn't mean that the company tolerates poor performance by individuals. Just the opposite is true. What it does mean is that managers are constantly analyzing failures, determining what processes need to be improved, and matching the right people to the right skill sets.

Being tough on issues, not on people, is a philosophy that goes beyond the obvious. Of course you don't yell at your team. But what about things that are not so obvious? Do you think much about how you're making people feel? Often our actions as managers have unintended consequences.

Consider this example: It's Friday afternoon and Joe and his assistant are finishing up an important presentation that he'll be giving on Monday. It needs a few more changes to be absolutely perfect. Joe knows exactly how he wants the changes to read and it probably wouldn't take him very long to do it himself, but his calendar is full. He turns it over to his assistant with a good-natured warning: "Don't spend too much time revising it. It shouldn't take more than about 30 minutes."

The weekend is fast approaching and suddenly the assistant is left to make "just a few changes" without knowing precisely how those changes should read. She rewords, which leads to more rewording and that leads to other changes and all of them need to be verified. Then, of course, all the page numbers change and that means more time at the copy machine. What Joe thinks will take just 30 minutes winds up taking hours. The assistant's weekend plans are ruined. Worse, Joe's assistant winds up feeling that she must be stupid because making the changes took so long, and she's not even sure Joe will like and approve of the changes. Joe, of course, is oblivious to all this and enjoys his weekend in the knowledge that his assistant has taken care of the minor revisions. Being tough on people takes many forms, some more obvious than others.

BUILDING WINNING TEAMS

Hiring the best people doesn't mean you'll get their best work. Little of consequence happens in business or even the public sector these days unless people come together to work in teams. People working collectively as a team are far more effective than the sum of their individual efforts and skills. That isn't news, but too many managers don't understand what teamwork means. It isn't simply assigning a diverse group to a project and setting a deadline. It requires each member of the team to tame his or her ego and ambition and become a partner with all the other team members, working for the good of the team by sharing information candidly and honestly and being willing, when necessary, to take a back-seat role.

The manager's job in molding an effective team is to evaluate every subordinate on his or her ability to join the team and participate fully, and to establish clear objectives and paths to success. Teamwork becomes a critical value, extending beyond any employee's individual domain skills. But it also requires that the manager be honest and candid with employees, individually and as a team, avoiding favoritism and making fair and honest decisions.

Taking a personal interest in each employee is part of the teamwork effort. It can be something as simple as calling them on their birthday to chat for a few minutes about how things are going or to discuss an idea, or it can become as complex as sponsoring an off-site retreat to brainstorm ideas for setting big goals for the team. If the team is functioning properly, it becomes possible for the manager to set higher standards, demanding excellence without being harsh. Team members want to be stretched and challenged.

Arnold had firsthand experience with what teams can accomplish when he headed the New Memphis Arena Public Building Authority (PBA) in 2001 as it set out to fulfill its agreement to build a new stadium for the Grizzlies, the Vancouver NBA team that moved to Memphis. The PBA's role was critical from the outset and that meant putting together the best possible team. Not only would it oversee construction of the arena, but would also work with other groups with absolute veto power during the process—the Memphis and Shelby County governments and the Grizzlies team. The team members not only had to trust each other, they had to earn the trust of a very skeptical voting public, many of whom had scant faith that an arena would be built within the timeframe and for the amount budgeted. To make matters worse, Arnold couldn't hand pick his team members. Two had to be local politicians and the rest—all Memphis business or civic leaders—were chosen by the Memphis mayor and his counterpart, the Shelby County mayor. Then everything required a blessing by a legislative body.

To align these diverse parties and make and execute decisions, Arnold and his team determined they had to keep things simple. The result was the small laminated red card that stated the principles around which the project would be based. The overall guideline—Build It Right—was followed by seven simple statements:

1. Assemble the best team.
2. On time and within budget.
3. Maximize minority participation.
4. Design it right.
5. Gain the public's trust.
6. Involve the community.
7. Exceed expectations.

The card's small size allowed everyone to carry a copy in their wallet or purse and the glaring red color caught the eye and ensured that the card wouldn't become just another wallet stuffer alongside unused credit cards or forgotten business cards. It seems simple and it was, but it worked. The team worked flawlessly to select architects and a lead contractor and to ensure that the project stayed on schedule.

Build It Right

- Assemble the best team
- On time and within budget
- Maximize minority participation
- Design it right
- Gain the public's trust
- Involve the community
- Exceed expectations

Staying on schedule wasn't easy. On July 22, 2003, a ferocious windstorm swept the Memphis area with winds exceeding 100 miles per hour. The wind severely damaged two of the three tower cranes working on the project. The largest crane was 252 feet tall and it was listing 19 feet from vertical. The only thing that prevented it from plummeting onto Beale Street, the heavily trafficked entertainment hub, was that it lay against the upper concourses of the arena. The windstorm could have been a project-busting disaster. But M.A. Mortenson Company, the primary contractor, responded immediately, flying in engineers and managers from other Mortenson projects as well as experts in damage assessment and rigging and hoisting equipment. The first challenge was to formulate a plan to secure the damaged cranes by raising them upright. Close inspection showed they were damaged beyond repair and had to be dismantled and removed from the site. An intricate web of cables, pulleys, and winches was set up to pull the cranes into position for the dismantling work. Then, rather than take the time to reconstruct replacement tower cranes, the firm brought in large mobile cranes. The mobile cranes necessitated changes in the plans for how to erect the massive steel framing of the arena roof. Altogether, the crane damage cost the project a total of 30 days, but Mortenson's swift response laid the groundwork to recover that lost time. By mid-December, changes in the construction plans, including a new sequence for fabricating and erecting the roof framing, had brought the massive project back onto schedule.

"I'm just a simple guy that expects to get results," says Dave Mansell, the project superintendent. "We did that through sheer determination. There never was a doubt in my mind that we would succeed. We had made a commitment to finish this project on time and we were not going to be deterred because of this act of Mother Nature."

For Arnold, Mansell embodied all the qualities one could hope for in a manager of a massive project. Mansell himself credits the success of the recovery effort to the stakeholders who had a common vision and a fierce determination and pride in getting the job done. As Arnold said publicly on many occasions, the PBA's selection of Mortenson was the key "difference maker" on this highly successful project.

ADVICE TO NEW MANAGERS

If you're in the early stages of your management career, there are some basic ideas that we want to pass on so perhaps you won't have to learn the hard way how to provide leadership to the people who work for you. As a manager, whether you know it or not, you're under constant scrutiny. Subordinates watch your every behavior and make decisions on department, team, or company values based on that behavior. Intense (but balanced) focus on the work and goals, seizing opportunities to learn more, and promoting subordinates' interaction with more senior executives or other leaders all are considered good by your subordinates. Not so good is sloppy behavior, even off the job, shifting blame, or criticizing others personally.

Subordinates also watch whom the manager hires, what skills are in demand, and what personalities are desired. They keep an eagle eye on how managers handle performance issues. Coddling those who don't measure up can destroy the morale of colleagues; likewise, dismissing or demoting a committed employee for reasons unrelated to performance can wreck a high-performing team and damage, if not destroy, the manager's credibility. Think about typical "boss behavior" as depicted in the cartoon strip Dilbert, which is certainly at odds with genuine people skills. "Bad" behavior takes the form of micromanaging, doing work that subordinates should do, and generally demoralizing those who should be learning by doing. Some managers bring in consultants to do work that would be an opportunity for employees to learn. Whether that's because the employees are incapable of doing it, or the manager lacks trust in their abilities, a problem exists. "Good" behavior takes the form of providing a vision for the completion of a project, clearly delineating roles and responsibilities, and leading positive and productive team sessions around milestones and performance gaps.

The Golden Rule can't be invoked too often in good management. If you don't treat others as you would like to be treated, you're likely to have some problems in the workplace. You want people to listen to you, but too often we forget that others want us to listen to them, too. You want to be able to approach people without fear of ridicule or humiliation. Your employees want to be able to approach you without fear, too. Sincerely respecting the dignity of employees means sharing performance concerns privately, showing them how to succeed, and reinforcing good results with rewards. But you also have to balance that with "tough love" when they make mistakes, confronting poor performance squarely and candidly, and making sure they aren't frustrated by flawed processes or conflicting goals. Just as you reward high performers, you must be willing to engage in adult conversations with nonperformers. Human nature often leads us to avoid conflict, but doing so merely delays success for all involved.

Self-awareness is a critical skill for managing people. How rooted in reality is your own impression of your management abilities? Perhaps you see yourself as a manager with a blend of people skills: compassion, identification with subordinates' professional (and personal) struggles and successes, a sincere concern for their welfare, consistently firm and decisive actions that do not coddle underperformers, and certainly a better-than-average understanding of the total business. All of us have some of those qualities. The key is to emphasize the right behaviors in the right situations. Those who can range among management styles can adapt well to the harsh and dynamic environment of business. Getting the right results the wrong way is not a recipe for longevity in your job. Screaming and threatening behavior may buy you results in the short term, but eventually, your employees will find ways to overcome such bullying, undermining you, or they will simply vote with their feet and head for greener pastures. An ideal manager is consistent, has a good command of functional skills (though others may have better), and demonstrates sincere interest in employees and their success. Just as important, the ideal manager gets the right results the right way—meeting goals regularly and innovating with positive change around process and output. Managing to the measurements—working to make sure the metrics reflect what management wants—is to flirt with disaster. The metrics are there to assess progress toward a given goal, and influencing them artificially without corresponding improvements to the underlying business takes away an important tool.

If we had to put our thoughts about managing people on a laminated card, here's what it would say:

Advice to New Managers

✔ Listen to your employees.

✔ Be approachable.

✔ Show sincere interest in your employees.

✔ Give and take feedback.

✔ Surround yourself with strong players.

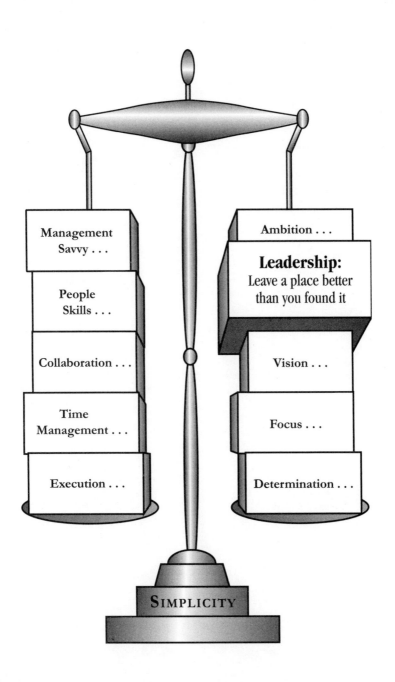

Management
Savvy . . .

People
Skills . . .

Collaboration . . .

Time
Management . . .

Execution . . .

Ambition . . .

Leadership:
Leave a place better
than you found it

Vision . . .

Focus . . .

Determination . . .

SIMPLICITY

CHAPTER 5

Leadership: Leave a Place Better than You Found It

The function of leadership is to produce more leaders, not more followers.

—Ralph Nader

The subject of leadership is probably the single most written about and discussed topic in all of management. Yet, it is also one of the most difficult challenges facing any manager. Just having a title of "manager" or "director" on your business card does not make you a leader. Becoming a leader requires a big leap and that's what this book is all about. If you are in a position of authority, your subordinates will, in most cases, do what you say. But are they willingly following your direction? Are you leading or just bossing? People are willing—even eager—to follow the direction of a leader because there is a quality about leaders that convinces others that following them is the right thing to do. We follow leaders because they know where they are going—or at least they make us think they do. Great leaders have the ability to quickly diagnose a situation and break it down into manageable solutions, and the ability to engage people in a productive way with excellent communication skills.

Leadership goes far beyond telling subordinates what to do. A great leader inspires the people who work for her to give their best effort, to stretch beyond the ordinary and to collaborate with each other.

Leadership grows out of two distinct power bases. One is organizational, usually reflected in your title which represents the authority to exercise leadership over the people who work for you. The second leadership power base is personal. Personal power is based on knowledge and expertise. People see you as a leader because you always seem to be the one with the knowledge, skills or expertise to solve a problem. Personal power may also be based on characteristics such as charisma and expressiveness. You're seen as a leader because your charisma draws people to you. They enjoy working with you and your ability to communicate builds strong bonds across the organization. No one can anoint you with the personal qualities of leadership. Most people have to develop them over time. You see these people every day. The next time you're in a meeting and a roadblock stops progress, you'll probably see one person toward whom everyone else will gravitate for an answer. It may not be the "official" person in charge in the meeting. Indeed, it may not even be a manager. But whenever this person says, "Here's what I think. . . ." everyone else in the room turns to listen. Pay attention next time— you're looking at a leader.

If you are lucky enough to combine both the organizational power base—the title of manager—and all of the traits and skills that give you a personal power base, you're in the right job. Unfortunately, some "leaders" have the title, but lack many or all of the necessary personality traits and skills to be a real leader. And, unfortunately, some true leaders go unnoticed because the ones with the title don't recognize what's right in front of them.

TICKETS TO PLAY

Leadership is a team discipline. It's all about the passion that inspires your team to work harder, think smarter, and follow where you lead willingly, not just because they have to. There are certain basic elements of leadership that are simply non-negotiable. They're what we call "tickets to play." Mastering these elements will provide you with a foundation for leadership. Simply put, they get you into the game.

Motivation

One of the first tickets to play is motivation. You've got to want to lead people to be an effective leader. You've also got to want to reach certain goals to be a leader. Without one of those two components—people to lead and a goal to lead them to—there's no point in leading. Examine your motives as a leader: Are you in this to get ahead? Do you want to be a leader in order to move up the corporate ladder? Are you a leader because you love interacting with people and have a knack for pulling together teams? Are you a leader because you have a clear vision of the future and you're full of energy and desire to share this vision and bring others along for the ride? True leadership emerges from caring deeply about the organization's goals and about the people you're leading toward those goals.

Competency

A second ticket to play is competency, proving that you can produce results. Leadership is earned by achieving results, excelling in your area, and gaining a track record for success. Leadership earned in this way establishes your authority to lead. It also makes you a valuable and respected resource for your team members. Proving your competency does *not* mean that you have to be able to do each job in your organization better than the person in that job. It does mean that you need to understand at a very deep level how your team members contribute toward achieving your organization's goals and how you can support them to produce the best possible results.

Trust and Respect

As a leader, you have to persuade your followers that they should follow you because they want to, not because they have to. The people you're leading must have respect for you as a leader. If they don't, you'll be leader in name only without a real following. Respect is one of those traits that takes a long time to build but can be destroyed very quickly. To earn your team's respect, your first step needs to be to respect them as individuals and as members of the team.

Trust is another key element of leadership. Trust is earned by demonstrating personal integrity: walking the talk. Your team will recognize whether your actions are congruent with your words. And in return for their trust, you need to trust your team members. First time managers often try to "micromanage" by monitoring everyone on their team, watching and even participating in every interaction and every communication, measuring how hard people are working, and noting how they are achieving results. A great leader is able to trust his or her team. He trusts their individual capabilities, he trusts that they are committed to the team's goals, and he is willing to let them find their own path in achieving these goals.

Trust is related to integrity. Integrity boils down to doing the right thing for the right reason. It's where your personal and corporate values become intertwined and transparent to everyone around you.

Willingness to Take Risks

A leader cannot afford to play it safe. Sticking with the status quo to avoid mistakes doesn't cut it in today's marketplace. At the same time, as a leader, you are no longer taking risks just for yourself, but for your entire team. That's a huge responsibility. Being a smart risk taker requires being savvy about which risks are worth it. You have to constantly ask yourself: "What would really make a difference to the organization?" Once defined, a great leader minimizes risk by obtaining buy-in for risky initiatives from across the organization. Being a leader doesn't have to be lonely. Finally, a great leader continuously monitors the effects of her decisions, keeping track of how things are going and being willing to revise her position if a decision turns out to have been a mistake.

TICKETS TO WIN

Tickets to play admit you to the management game. But if you want to be an exceptional manager, you don't settle for just playing. You want to win. The following "tickets to win" can help separate you from the pack.

Transparency

Have you heard the expression "information is power"? Some managers hoard information because they believe it strengthens their power base. They share information only on an "as needed" basis. They discourage broad and open communication within and across their teams. They especially try to keep a lid on what is communicated beyond their own organization. Any information to their superiors needs to flow through them. Any communication to the "outside" needs to be vetted by them.

In contrast to this, great leaders lead with transparency, or "Open Kimono." They share information broadly across their organization. They provide access to their team to other leaders in the company, including their own bosses. Leading "Open Kimono" means everyone on a team, as well as those outside the team, knows what the goals and priorities are, how well the plan to achieve them is being executed, and who's doing their part and who isn't. Together the team takes ownership of its performance. Scorecards are useful devices to provide a highly visible traffic-light motif of green, yellow, and red symbols next to a numeric assessment. The team always and instantly knows if it is behind, on schedule or in a danger zone. By displaying emerging successes and shortfalls, a team can energize itself to fix problems and even to attract collaboration from colleagues outside the team to turn around performance shortfalls.

Courage

You won't stand out as a leader unless you're willing to take risks and make some hard decisions. Taking risks requires courage, the second ticket to win. Great leaders show courage in many ways: they are willing to stand up for their beliefs, even if they're unpopular; they don't avoid conflict but have the courage to resolve interpersonal issues directly; they have the courage to risk failure. To grow as a leader, you need to operate slightly beyond your comfort zone.

Visualize the Future

Leaders who distinguish themselves can see the future. This doesn't involve crystal balls or magic. It's simply the ability to use your knowledge of the business and the world in which it operates to look far ahead and prepare for challenges and opportunities that may arise. Years ago, FedEx began looking at the opportunities to do business in China. Back then China wasn't the economic powerhouse that it has become in the last few years and the opportunities for business were very limited. But having a presence there, gaining knowledge about how the culture and economy worked, paid dividends later when suddenly China threw open its doors and welcomed foreign businesses.

Decisiveness

In business, as in life, there are people who dread or delay making decisions. They invariably claim the delay is because they don't have enough information, need more feedback, or have to perform more analysis. But the truth is, delaying decisions to be able to find the "perfect answer" just isn't a realistic or good way to do business. And if you wait, your competitor will probably have already acted and you'll likely be the loser. Subconsciously, the underlying fear is: "What if it's the wrong decision? I'll be blamed." There are two possibilities—that you will make a well-reasoned, carefully assessed but swiftly executed decision, and the outcome is a good one, or you'll make a less-than-stellar decision and have to explain it. Though the latter may seem like the end of the world, it is not. If your decision was made based on reliable analysis and for the right reasons, accept the responsibility for the outcome and learn from the mistake. Leadership-oriented bosses value managers who are willing to act decisively—working from good information, of course—and will recognize that you're growing into your job.

On the flip side, there is the equally problematic issue of making decisions far too quickly. These judgments usually are based on "gut instincts" without sufficient information. You might get lucky a few times, but one day you'll make a big mistake and it will be painfully evident in the aftermath that you simply didn't know what you were doing. Again, the best path is to have confidence, take in enough information, and act on it swiftly.

Evangelization

Evangelization is the ability to influence people over whom you have no authority. A great leader is always on the lookout for opportunities to be an ambassador for his team and its goals. Tom practices evangelization constantly, both within his team and with those colleagues his team serves. In his division, the concept of evangelization plays a huge role. In contrast to more traditional functions like sales or marketing or operations, FedEx Solutions as a function is not self-explanatory. It took being an ambassador for his team, both within FedEx and outside FedEx, to ensure all the parties understood what FedEx Solutions does.

Evangelization was a key part of Arnold's strategy as he worked to make the FedExForum a success. For example, he handed out more than 1,000 of his now-famous Red Cards, not to mention his countless speaking engagements and media interviews. Arnold laughs as he says he continually harped—probably ad nauseam—on the core principle "On Time and Within Budget." That evangelization paid off when the principle became firmly fixed in the minds of all team members involved in building the FedExForum. Arnold and his PBA colleagues gambled that they could build it on time and on budget and evangelized that principle throughout. But they could have set themselves up for failure, especially given the history of constructing large public building projects that typically come in wildly late and way over budget. But the determination to succeed was fueled by their evangelization efforts, which, Arnold says, practically willed the project into being a success.

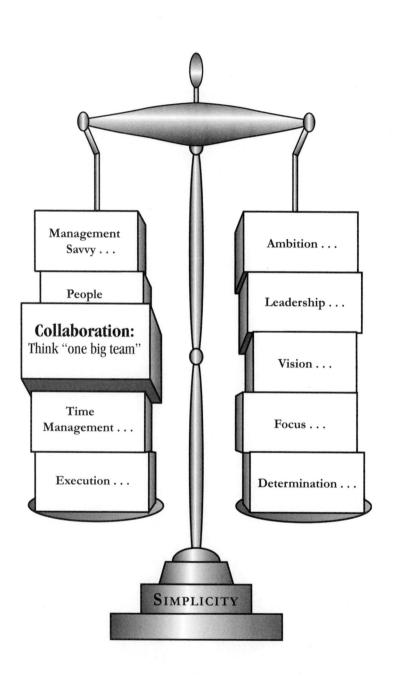

Management
Savvy . . .

People

Collaboration:
Think "one big team"

Time
Management . . .

Execution . . .

Ambition . . .

Leadership . . .

Vision . . .

Focus . . .

Determination . . .

SIMPLICITY

CHAPTER 6

Collaboration: Think "One Big Team"

*If you have an apple and I have an apple and we
exchange these apples then you and I will still each
have one apple. But if you have an idea and I
have an idea and we exchange these ideas, then
each of us will have two ideas.*

—George Bernard Shaw

The seemingly effortless teamwork that we see in
professional football, basketball, or baseball doesn't
just happen. The players in those sports are skilled
people in their own right, but they also function in a
highly synchronized way to achieve their mutual goal.
If you look past their dazzling prowess, what you will
see is really the result of the coach's ability to get the
players to collaborate. The same principles apply in
setting up great business teams.

When we talk about collaboration and teamwork
we aren't confining ourselves to our own teams. Collaboration extends across the functional silos and even

beyond the confines of your company to include customers and suppliers. Basically, collaboration occurs any time two or more people decide to work together as a group, submerging their own egos for the benefit of the project at hand.

Effective collaboration doesn't just happen, it has to be managed. As a leader, you have to take the initiative to ensure that it does. The easiest and most productive use of collaboration comes within your own team. You serve as the coach and have the authority, if necessary, to ensure that your team members cooperate and that they "play well with others."

THE PRINCIPLES OF COLLABORATION

Collaboration occurs among people only when they accept the concept. To ensure that the process is a good experience rather than a bad one, certain principles must be kept in mind.

Mutual Respect

Collaboration starts with mutual respect. The people with whom you wish to collaborate have to respect you. They need to know that if they share information, opinions, and even emotions, they aren't at risk of losing credit for their successful ideas or being ridiculed for ideas that don't work. At the same time, you must respect the people with whom you're collaborating. Mutual respect is based on the belief that everyone in a collaborative effort has valuable contributions to make; everyone brings something important to the table; and each person's ideas, opinions, and input matter. Without this ingredient, what appears to be a collaboration is nothing more than keeping people "in the loop"—letting others know what you're up to, without expecting or really desiring their input.

Enthusiasm

Knowledge and skill should be a given for anyone with whom you collaborate. Yet all too often the enthusiasm factor is overlooked, even though it is one of the most necessary traits for a team member to have. Over the years we've become very wary of people who purport to be part of a team, but who constantly play the "devil's advocate" by suggesting why some problem can't be solved or some goal achieved. Someone playing this role may regard himself as a smart contributor who points out obstacles that others don't see. But too often these devil's advocates are really just naysayers, looking only for reasons not to do something, rather than looking for ways to overcome hurdles. A single person articulating the reasons

113

something can't be done is enough to bring an entire project to a grinding halt.

Focusing on team members who bring a can-do attitude does not mean surrounding yourself with a lot of "yes" people who agree to anything and everything, without thinking about the process of accomplishing a goal or solving a problem. Every team needs to understand that the path to each goal has barriers that need to be overcome. But there is a difference between an underlying attitude of negativity and one of "we can do it; now let's figure out together how to overcome the obstacles."

Inclusiveness

Inclusiveness is another bedrock principle of collaboration. If you start a project by including all the people who will eventually have a role in it, the chances grow immeasurably that the project will be completed on time and on budget. This isn't to say that you have to hold a meeting of 100 people just to launch a new initiative. But many managers forget that at some point in the process a project is going to require input from other functions (for example, legal, finance, and human resources). Rather than waiting until the project is nearly completed to get the necessary signoffs, why not bring those departments into the process at the beginning? Not only does that pave the way for future approval (they aren't "surprised" at the last minute and forced to make a snap judgment), but it also brings more intellectual firepower to the table. Some managers think of legal, finance, or human resources as "blockers" and try to avoid them until the end of the decision-making process. True collaboration is based on mutual respect. It means looking at these groups as savvy business people with a unique and valuable perspective.

BARRIERS TO COLLABORATION

If collaboration is such a great thing, why don't more managers do it? Just as the principles we just discussed encourage collaboration, there are also common barriers to collaboration of which a leader needs to be aware.

Unwillingness to Share Power

Among the most important and prevalent barriers is an unwillingness to share power. The very nature of collaboration is to share credit. Many aggressive, gung-ho managers will see this as a bad thing. They think in terms of zero-sum games, in which any advance one person makes is at the cost of another person. Their rationale runs something like this: If I can grab all the credit, I'll get ahead faster, so I shouldn't place myself in a position in which I have to share credit.

The fallacy of that kind of thinking can be shown by comparing it to a baseball game. Strike one occurs when the uncooperative individual achieves less than what could have been accomplished through collaboration. Strike two occurs when senior managers review the performance of this individual and his manager. If the word gets around at higher levels that you aren't a team player, chances are your grab for all the credit will wind up causing you to strike out for the third time, costing you that "corporate" home run.

"Pretend" Collaboration

Managers who are not team players may realize that they're being judged in part on their willingness and ability to collaborate with others in the company. In order to appear "collaborative," they cite some people outside their own department in an email to a superior or they mention another department in a speech about their initiative. It certainly looks and sounds like they're collaborating. In reality, they are only creating the impression of collaboration, while at the same time busily building barriers to true collaboration. An occasional memo or email copied to another function is not truly inviting or valuing their input. Rather, it's just an example of "pretend" collaboration.

Narrow Scorecards

Finally, the way in which companies measure performance can discourage collaboration. It is very tempting for a manager assigning responsibilities to be very narrow and specific when determining objectives or setting up scorecards. After all, specificity should lead to focus and clear delineation of responsibilities. But that very narrowness allows a person to claim that he was successful in his role, even if the entire project comes crashing down in ruins. Managers need to promote collaboration by setting broader mandates and holding every participant responsible not for just a small segment of a project, but for the overall success of the entire project.

LEVELS OF COLLABORATION

Collaboration shouldn't be limited to your own team of direct reports, but should extend throughout the company and even beyond the bounds of the company to include customers and suppliers. Let's take a look at what collaboration at each of those three levels means.

Collaboration within a Team

The easiest and most productive use of collaboration comes within your own team. You serve as the coach and have the authority, if necessary, to ensure that your team members cooperate (again, that they "play well with others"). Tom has three departments reporting to him, each led by a competitive, results-oriented, and highly effective leader. Some time ago it became apparent that all three departments were functioning extremely well on their own initiatives and projects, but they weren't collaborating much. Each of the three department heads was focused on what his department was achieving and wasn't concerned about what was happening elsewhere, nor about what effect this was having on the entire division.

That's when Tom summoned his three managers to what has become known within the division as the "Bonne Terre Conference." During two days of sometimes heated, sometimes painful discussions at Bonne Terre, an idyllic conference center bed-and-breakfast south of Memphis, Tom laid out his vision of what collaboration within the division should look like. Then, the three department heads and their staffs identified the problems that stood in the way of Tom's vision. With the help of a facilitator, they identified very specifically where communication and collaboration were breaking down. They began to realize that becoming an outstanding division within

FedEx would not be achieved by squeezing an additional 5 percent out of each of their own initiatives. They had to figure out problems together and actively look for linkages, rather than grudgingly keeping the rest of the division informed.

At first this two-day offsite meeting seemed like an incredible waste of time. But when the session broke up and everyone drove home to Memphis, the groundwork for collaboration had been laid. Formal guidelines were established that analyzed each department and designated who should be collaborating with whom on what projects. The formal guidelines were reinforced by Tom's continuing evangelization that if one department won at the expense of another, it really wasn't a win, but a loss for the division as a whole. Finally, Tom made collaboration one of the goals in his team's management objectives and on the division's scorecard.

Companywide Collaboration

Breaking down silos that exist outside your span of control can be even more of a challenge than leveling those within your own team. It's a task that requires persuasion and logic. The first step is to find a simple, but descriptive, articulation of your initiative. The second step is to identify the internal contributors and stakeholders whose input is necessary for the successful execution of the project and invite them to join the team. The third step is continuous evangelization about why this effort is so important and why their contributions matter. This is accompanied by well-documented scorecard "evidence" showing the progress being made. The benefits are many. Obviously the project at hand gets the focus it needs from the right parties. Additionally, by enlisting the aid of groups outside your own immediate circle, you set a precedent and build relationships that will make working with these formerly siloed groups much easier in the future. More importantly, you reinforce the idea that everyone *is* on the same team, working to make the organization as a whole successful and profitable.

Collaboration across Companies

In a supplier-customer relationship, there is a tendency to think in terms of zero-sum games that steer your company and your customer or supplier away from collaboration and into so-called "arm's-length" transactions. We're gratified to note a small but growing trend in business-to-business relations toward what is called "collaborative selling" or "solution selling." Those are fancy words for what amounts to teamwork between two separate companies. Just as teamwork in your own department or your own company requires respect for one another, collaborative selling requires that the selling company and the buy-ing company respect and trust one another. At the heart of collaborative selling is the customer's willing-ness to share large amounts of data and to describe, openly and candidly, the nature of the problems it faces. Only then can the seller begin to fashion a real solution, rather than simply offer a product or service tailored to meet the customer's needs. In exchange for devising a solution, the seller can expect to re-ceive a premium price, albeit not so high as to de-stroy the value of the solution to the customer. In the end, this kind of collaborative relationship becomes a competitive advantage to both the buyer and the seller, a true "win-win" situation.

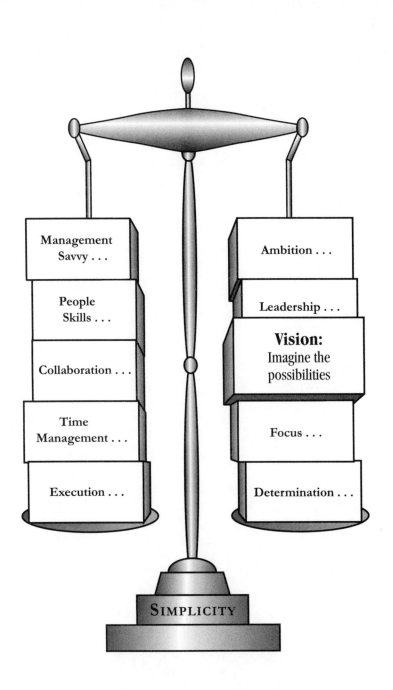

CHAPTER 7

Vision: Imagine the Possibilities

If you want to build a ship, don't herd people together to collect wood and don't assign them tasks and work, but rather teach them to long for the endless immensity of the sea.

—Antoine de Saint-Exupery

The "daily grind" is all about solving new and un-expected problems, attending meetings, answering questions, writing reports. The myriad things that occupy our time seem to go on forever. Everyone is so caught up with what's going to happen in the next five days or even the next five hours that they seldom have the time or inclination to think about what might be happening five years from now. Yet the pace of change is accelerating every day, and companies must change rapidly or be left behind. That's why it is becoming increasingly important that middle and senior managers find time amid the daily bustle to envision what the future will look like.

Jeff Immelt, the chairman of GE, sponsors what he calls "Dream Sessions" several times each year. These are meetings between GE managers and the managers of one of GE's big customers in such industries as power generation or airlines. The agenda is passed around long before the two-day sessions begin to give everyone time to prepare. The idea is to look far into the future to see what shape that particular industry will be taking. What technologies will be in place? Who will be the new competitors? What new products or services will be needed? Since it's the future the participants are discussing, no one can state with any certainty what the answers to those questions will be. But identifying the issues and trends that could be taking place five years out gets everyone thinking and planning for the long-term future. GE itself uses those sessions to determine how it allocates some of its research-and-development funds.

Even if you can't spare two days to follow Immelt's lead, you can create an equally productive subset of his approach—maybe a quick lunch with a customer or supplier to talk about new trends or changes. And you can do the same thing in meetings with employees or colleagues. Central to the idea is learning what you and your team can begin doing now that will help you execute better in the future.

THE FEDEX VISION

The very name FedEx conjures up images of board-room success and Fortune 500 environments where speed is of the essence and yesterday's news is just that. Pick up any business school textbook and you'll see references to FedEx and its legendary founder, Frederick W. Smith. That isn't surprising considering that he did what others only dream about—he invented an industry and built it into one of the most powerful companies in the world. He built something we didn't even know we needed and turned it into a household word. He put purple and orange together and told us it looked good. And it does.

A single vision can launch an industry, but it takes continuous long-term vision for a company to remain innovative and competitive. A vision that is critical to FedEx's continuing success is that information about a package's transit status is nearly as important as the package itself. Anything that has to be delivered overnight with a guarantee is important enough that the sender wants to know it got through. That's how package tracking developed and it has expanded today to notification to a recipient that a package is on the way—often before the recipient is even aware that someone is sending him something.

The expansion of Smith's original vision has been continuous. Today, FedEx has an unsurpassed worldwide network, with operating companies that independently offer flexible, specialized services that represent the broadest array of supply chain, transportation, business, and related information services.

Sometimes realizing a vision takes time. Part of Smith's vision years ago was a FedEx that served the world's biggest country—China. With his uncanny knack of skating to where the puck will be, Smith knew the importance of gaining a foothold in China and as early as 1984 had begun putting in place the critical elements needed to provide consistent express freight and document transport. Because of that foresight, FedEx was already well positioned to do business when the Chinese government began to switch gears in the 1990s to grow the country's economy and become an economic powerhouse. FedEx now serves 190 cities in China, and plans to expand service to 100 additional cities within the next five years. FedEx provides reliable pickup and delivery, international line-haul using its own aircraft to link China to the extensive FedEx regional and global networks, and rapid customs clearance. Today many companies are developing market strategies in China, but they're reactionary, not visionary. Meanwhile FedEx is already on to the next big challenge.

Going beyond "Do-Able"

Developing a true breakthrough vision means not being limited to "what is do-able" but stretching the boundaries of what is deemed possible. Seeing a vision through to reality often requires both persistence and collaboration. As aircraft grew in size over the past decades and as it added more to its fleet to accommodate increasing volumes, FedEx found itself limited in its Memphis hub location. The longest runway at Memphis Airport was 9,000 feet. That wasn't enough to accommodate the takeoff runs of the biggest aircraft flying to Europe fully loaded. But the Memphis-Shelby County Airport Authority had a vision of being the largest cargo airport in the world and wasn't about to lose that goal because a runway was too short.

You might think building a new runway amounts to backing up a truck and pouring some concrete. Far from it. On average, it takes 10 years from the time planning begins for a new airport runway to the day that the first airplane lands on the newly paved surface. The decision to lengthen the runway touched off a huge planning and construction project that began with the construction of a parallel runway that would handle the existing air traffic while the old runway was extended and resurfaced. Simply building the parallel runway involved considerations about changes in the noise patterns of aircraft that affected many of the adjoining neighborhoods, relocating a seasonal stream that affected water quality and wildlife habitat, preparing a financing plan that was fair and equitable for the different classes of airport users, and managing a complex and busy airfield during a major construction project.

The project succeeded because the Memphis-Shelby County Airport Authority has as one of its guiding principles to maintain a culture of collaborative relationships with airlines, tenants, government agencies, and other airport stakeholders. That collaborative mindset made it possible for out-of-the-box thinking to solve the many problems that occurred during the more than 10 years it took to complete this important project. In 2000, the airport's 11,100-foot "World Runway" and the associated heavy-duty taxiways opened for aircraft.

DOING THINGS DIFFERENTLY

The first step in formulating a vision is understanding change. A vision of the future is a vision of how things can be done differently. Think of change as a totally different use for a product, the identification of another company that could become a collaborator on a new initiative, or even a new internal structure to accomplish things differently. Change is part of the structure of business and it's your job to recognize that change will be continuous and that it isn't a barrier. Instead, by taking advantage of change to make continuous improvements, change becomes a competitive advantage. The next step is to translate your vision for change into actionable goals.

Developing a vision for the company is not just a job for the CEO or senior management or a strategic planning department. It is everyone's responsibility to figure out what is "coming down the pike." Often the best intelligence that leads to a well-informed vision comes from front-line employees—sales professionals who are out in front of customers, customer service representatives who talk to customers and learn what they like and don't like or manufacturing employees who know what parts break easily. Developing a vision should become a dialogue, with ideas being pushed up and down the hierarchy. A key component of visioning is questioning the status quo. Often, questioning the status quo requires getting away from the everyday pressures and current business problems. This is why off-site meetings, sometimes called retreats, can be very effective. With a proper agenda prepared in advance and a skilled facilitator, whether you or someone else, a meeting away from the office, phones, and email can be amazingly productive in terms of new ideas and initiatives. It can also give you a chance to see another side of your team members. You may be surprised at who blossoms in this less hectic and intimidating environment, contributing ideas that neither you nor they realized were floating around the office unarticulated and thus useless.

In order to be a leading-edge company, you need to continuously keep your vision ahead of current facts. Great leaders always ask, "What's next?"

There was a time not too long ago when a sales force could merely memorize product offerings and prices and could offer a quote to a customer with just a few scribblings on a lunch table napkin. But as the complexity of offerings increases, few sales people are going to be able to keep all that information in their heads. It's imperative that the structure of the sales department changes so that the sales people don't necessarily know all the information, but they do know where to get it and how to put it together. In other words, you're flipping a switch from learning things by heart to accessing knowledge. It's just another variant of the old saying: Give a man a fish and he eats for one day; teach a man to fish and he eats for the rest of his life. By giving the sales force access to a large volume of information, they can envision customized solutions for their customers that wouldn't have been possible a decade ago.

ANCHORING YOUR VISION

Anchoring your vision means to act as if the future is now. What do we mean by that? In Tom's organization at FedEx, the focus has been on supporting the company's sales efforts in the United States. That's been remarkably successful and is something the entire team can be proud of having accomplished. But Tom's vision for the sales support organization and his team's mission is global. It's going to take a while to get there. But by *acting* as if sales support already is a global function, his team has already begun thinking that way. Tom has set in place an anchoring mechanism that converts the vision to the reality.

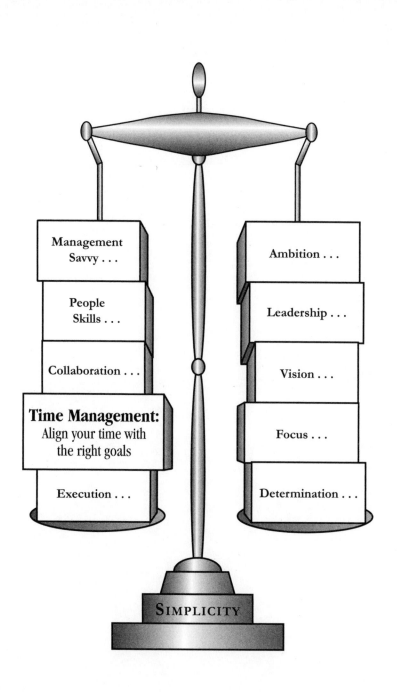

CHAPTER 8

Time Management: Align Your Time with the Right Goals

Dost thou love life? Then do not squander time,
for that is the stuff life is made of.

—Benjamin Franklin

Time is a big deal at FedEx. The company built its reputation on delivering packages and documents quickly and reliably. Ask any FedEx courier and they'll not only know the time, but also how much of it they have left in the countdown. But there's another way to think about what FedEx does. It was articulated recently by Rob Carter, the company's chief information officer, in an interview with *Fortune* magazine. The *Fortune* writer asked Rob, "What business is FedEx in?"

"I believe we engineer time," Rob said. "I believe that as the world shrinks and changes, we offer solutions that allow you to engineer time to make things happen along time schedules that weren't possible."

141

As Rob's take on FedEx and engineering time suggests, this chapter isn't a traditional time management guide telling you how to find a few minutes more here or there or how to squeeze in one more task in your already overwhelming day. Rather, it's about using time as a strategic resource. Indeed, time is probably the single most valuable asset that any company has and—like any asset—its value can decrease when not used efficiently.

TIME MANAGEMENT OF A DIFFERENT KIND

Some people are surprised to learn Tom uses timesheets for the employees in his FedEx division. Timesheets? Didn't those disappear shortly after the Industrial Revolution? The answer has nothing to do with how many hours of work Tom expects from each of his employees in a day, week, or month. Rather, the timesheets tell Tom and everyone who works for him if they're putting their time into the things that really matter. This information is crucial for three reasons. First, he wants to make sure that his division supports the corporation's current fiscal year core objectives. His employees use timesheets to track how much time they spend on initiatives that support those objectives. This tells Tom whether or not he is allocating enough of his resources—people and the time they have to do their jobs—to the right things. The timesheets give him a picture of that time allocation.

Second, the timesheet helps Tom track how well his division serves its internal customers, the divisions or other operating companies that provide funding to his team in exchange for assistance. Tom updates his division's internal customers regularly and his timesheets help him show the amount of time his team spends on their projects. Tom's counterparts on these teams can see at a glance that their support dollars are well spent.

Finally, the timesheets play an important role as "red flags" to tell Tom when resources are becoming too strained. He knows then that he has the data to build a case for hiring more team members.

"Timesheets are not about telling each person they need to squeeze out two more things this week," he explains. "Tracking time is about using time as a strategic resource. It allows me to keep a finger on the pulse of my division, to be sure I'm moving the needle in the right direction. I want to be sure that I spend a good part of my time on content issues that we need to resolve, a good part of my time on people issues—helping them grow or overcome challenges—and a good part of my time making sure I connect with my internal and external partners."

Timesheets are not just a tool for executives. They can help anyone who uses them ensure that he or she is spending their time wisely by focusing on the most important issues. They are a means for aligning timeshare with mindshare. This isn't trivial. Studies show that many managers, and consequently their teams, spend too much time on trivial or non-essential tasks that have little to do with the organization's overall mission. We challenge you to keep a timesheet for a week and analyze where your time and efforts are going.

GETTING TO WHAT'S IMPORTANT

We'll be the first to acknowledge that managing your time effectively is a tough nut to crack. Think about your typical day. You're up before dawn, scanning the newspaper while listening to CNBC or some other source of news. In the car, the radio is reporting more news, unless, of course, you have it turned down so you can talk about business on your cell phone. At the office, you're probably a few minutes late to the 9 A.M. meeting because you had two urgent telephone calls to return, and the human resources person caught you in the hall to remind you that you're two days overdue with those performance reviews. If you're lucky, you can sit uninterrupted in the meeting for an hour, although that really isn't an hour well spent since half of the meeting is spent reviewing decisions already made and talking about issues that are irrelevant to you. So, you sneak looks at email on your handheld device until the meeting adjourns. Then, it's back to your office and the phone, returning calls, answering questions, finding out information, all with the telephone receiver clamped firmly between neck and shoulder so you'll be hands free to answer the most urgent emails (the less urgent ones you relegate to the afternoon—hoping you'll have some time then).

How in the world do you ever get anything done?

Relax. You're not alone. This chaos is, in large part, the nature of business. What you can do is take some steps to smooth the flow, carve out blocks of time for quiet reflection and use your time, and that of others, more effectively and efficiently. The specific methods and tools we're laying out in the rest of this chapter are there for you to adapt to your own situation. Take what works for you, toss out the rest and get on with the job.

Even senior executives get the same 24 hours in a day as the rest of us. So how does Tom fit everything he has to do into that time span? Easy—he's got a system that works for him. His system focuses on compartmentalizing his "to do" list and then working in what he calls "blocks." He does his email at the end of the day instead of haphazardly fitting in one or two while he's doing other things. He also takes a breather at the end of the day.

"I go home, talk to Petra—just hang out, and we talk about our day. I work out, then I'm feeling refreshed and I go back in later to do some more work."

Tom is known for his responsiveness and he'll answer just about all of his emails. His direct reports learn quickly what kinds of email he thinks are time wasters. For example, do not—whatever you do—send him an email just to tell him you got *his* email.

"Unless we're having a major email server crisis, I am going to assume the recipient got the email."

But ask him for input or ask a question and you can count on an answer. And because he schedules emails at more or less the same time each day, his team also learns when to look for those answers. You'll hear them say, "Well, I didn't get my answer in the 6 P.M. block—he'll probably get back to me in the second shift (9 P.M. or later)."

Tom also believes in letting people stand for their own work. He adds what value he can, then the ball goes back across the net to the other player. That serves two purposes. First, it doesn't put another item on his own list and second, it gives the team member some ownership.

PRIORITIES

More efficient use of your time requires a more stringent approach toward setting priorities. If this seems like an obvious recommendation, consider this: While many people *set* priorities, they don't often *follow* them. Instead, they get caught up in things that could or should be done by other people or they get sidetracked by meaningless tasks to the exclusion of things that are absolutely critical, jobs only they can do.

Of course you can't prioritize everything you do. Can you imagine assessing the priority of every email or carefully weighing the phone call from the aggrieved customer judging whether it is low enough on your priority list that you can afford to safely pass it off to a subordinate? Some tasks can be completed in the time it would take to prioritize them. But you *can* think about your overall activities, your "regular" activities, and assign them a priority. We've included a tool to make it easy for you. Take a look at the four priorities in the following grid.

Urgent and Important

In this section you should include:

- Emergencies
- Deadline-driven projects
- Problems that require immediate action

These are must-do tasks that need to be completed at once. Because these tasks are urgent, you should deal with them first. They are also important, so you should devote as much time and effort to them as you can.

Important, Not Urgent

In this section you should include:

- Planning
- Relationship building
- Networking
- Personal development
- Identifying new opportunities

These are often the preferred tasks—the ones you would rather do first because they tend to be more interesting. Don't ignore these tasks, but try to set some time aside each day to work on them. If they are left too long, these tasks can become urgent.

Urgent, Not Important

In this section you should include:

- Interruptions
- Some phone calls or emails
- Some meetings
- Dealing with other people's concerns

As these tasks are urgent you do need to deal with them. The key is not to spend too much time on them. They may be urgent but they are not important to you personally, so deal with them as quickly as you can and move on.

Not Urgent, Not Important

In this section you should include:

- Things that you might prefer to do
- Social conversations with colleagues
- Dealing with junk mail
- Direct marketing letters
- Other time wasters

These are tasks that should be given the least priority. Do these tasks only when you have nothing more important to do.

Urgent and Important

All of these tasks are important, you say. Of course they are—but they're not all urgent. Take another look and ask yourself which ones are urgent and have to be done now. Those are the ones you deal with first. Some of them are going to be emergencies—events which by definition don't come with any preplanning. Shifting gears to attack items in this category requires the flexibility to throw out your agenda for the day and think and act in the here and now.

Important but Not Urgent

These are the tasks that have perhaps the biggest impact on the business and handling them will require some effort on your part. Among the tasks that fit into this category are planning, relationship building, identifying new threats or opportunities, and personal development. They're not urgent if you plan well and take care of them in an orderly, organized fashion. But if you let some of these tasks, such as planning and identifying threats, slip too long without attention, they are likely to become both important *and* urgent. This could have a huge impact on your team. And, face it, if your team is not delivering on its objectives, chances are it will have an impact on your internal customers and their

149

objectives. In the end, it will contribute to a bigger-picture negative impact to the organization's overall business plan.

What about the "warm and fuzzy" tasks, like relationship building and personal development? Obviously these don't have the same high-visibility repercussions if they get relegated to the back burner like the Important/Urgent and other Important/Not Urgent tasks. It's all too easy when the time pressure hits to look at your calendar and say, "I'm going to skip that lunch today with the marketing director for new product development. I can't spare the time with this huge customer implementation launching tomorrow." So you send a "cancel meeting notice" explaining your current crisis. She understands and probably is relieved. After all, she's got her own set of crises.

All's well that ends well, right? You managed that little chunk of time well, right? Well, not necessarily. If you continually postpone the subtle, yet important areas of building bridges with other departments or keep putting off working on components of your personal development plan, you are short-circuiting your business savvy growth. You are setting limitations on your ability to be the best that you can be. Guess what this does for your ability to compete for increased responsibilities when new management opportunities arise?

Urgent but Not Important

Here's the category that drives most of us nuts. It those irritating interruptions, those nonessential phone calls and emails. It's those "why am I here?" meetings. Many managers spend the majority of their workday in this box. The biggest sources for these tend to be colleagues whose "Urgent and Important" quadrant matches more closely to your "Important but Not Urgent" designation. Their urgent needs aren't particularly important to you and hearing about them keeps you from tasks that you do consider to be important. Too many people let the urgency of other peoples' tasks command their attention and waste their time.

Not Urgent and Not Important

If you've nothing else to do, this is the stuff you deal with. And when was the last time you had nothing else to do? Exactly. These are things you shouldn't waste time doing or even thinking about.

DELEGATION

Delegation sounds simple enough. After all, it's just assigning tasks to members of your team. Good delegation, however, is actually a fine art. Good

Prioritization: Case Study

Jane was a sales director at a midsized manufacturing firm. She had worked her way up the ranks and now managed a team of about a dozen sales reps. She was also responsible for her company's presence at trade shows and had recently volunteered to mentor a young female "rising star" in the organization. Jane was known as a hard worker, efficient at getting things done, and highly reliable. Her boss, Bob, knew he could count on her when things got tough, and her team admired her leadership.

The day began much like any other day. In the morning Jane held her weekly staff meeting and, as usual, the team discussed upcoming customer meetings and sales trends. Overall sales had been somewhat slack in recent months, and Jane's team had been given a stretch goal for new customer acquisitions. It was regarded as very important by senior management.

During the meeting, Jane got an urgent page from Bob: need to meet ASAP! A major customer had called Bob, irate about a billing error. Jane cut the meeting short. The only item remaining on the agenda was the preparation of a presentation for senior management on the new customer initiative, which she delegated to Peter, one of her most experienced sales people.

152

Jane spent most of the rest of the day tracking down the purchasing director at the customer site, clarifying the issue with billing and keeping Bob up to date on her progress. During her brief lunch, she met with Anne, whom she was mentoring. Anne was very grateful for her help and support and Jane enjoyed their conversation. In the afternoon, she checked in with Peter, who seemed well on track with the presentation. She told him to forward it to Bob when he was done.

At five in the afternoon, Jane left to pick up her four-year-old son from childcare and was looking forward to her evening. She felt good about the day and the various tasks she had juggled. When she got home there was a message on her answering machine. Bob, quite annoyed, had reviewed the presentation and had found several errors in it. He wanted her to call back right away.

How would you classify Jane's tasks using the priority matrix?

Did her time management match her priorities?

What "mistakes" did she make?

If you consider expectation management as a task—where does this fall in the priority matrix and how well did she do?

Should Jane call Bob back that night? What are her alternatives? What can she learn from this day?

delegation doesn't mean just assigning a task. It means assigning it to the right person and then trusting that person to do it. In other words, the manager needs to let go. If you cannot do that, you will micromanage your team, killing any personal initiative and enthusiasm. On the flip side is a manager whose first instinct is to assign tasks to team members without further ado. A "Please handle" is about the extent of the contribution in a hurriedly forwarded email. There is a happy medium between the micromanaging leader and one who takes the easy way out and delegates with no input whatsoever.

Managers who are on their way to becoming leaders have learned the art of delegation but know just how far to step back. To achieve that balance, ask yourself where and how you can add value in the stream of activities. If you get an email that generates work, the only choices aren't (a) just do it yourself, or (b) immediately forward it on to someone on your team. The leader adds value. The leader might append some suggestions or an idea on where to get input, before forwarding this to a team member. The leader then trusts that employee to do the work. That doesn't mean you cannot check in after a while. After all, that's another opportunity to add value.

Ultimately, you will want to build a team that you trust enough to allow expanding your range of delegation. When you have that high-performing team, you'll feel comfortable asking someone to email senior management—even the CEO—and you won't ask to see it first. You can be assured that team member will put extra care into that piece of work, and the exposure you provide and trust you place in that employee will serve you well in the end.

As you think about your responsibilities in the context of adding value and delegation, you can begin to classify them into several buckets:

- ✔ Best if I do
- ✔ Best if someone else does
- ✔ Best if left alone

Best if I Do

These are the things that no one else can do for you. These are items where you have a lot of value to add, your expertise is needed and where delegation would create more rework than it's worth. It's too easy to fall into the "takes too long to explain to someone else" trap of classifying most of your tasks into this category. If you're in this trap, you're underutilizing your team. If there are too many things you feel you're better off doing yourself, you either have the wrong people working for you, or haven't taken the time to coach them on how to get things done.

Best if Someone Else Does

If you've assembled a team of people whose skills complement your own and are clear on how they fall into the will-skill matrix (see Chapter 4) then the decision of when and to whom to delegate becomes easy. As simple as it sounds, getting this right is the key to a high-performing team, one in which everyone eagerly embraces his or her responsibilities, collaborates where necessary, shares instead of hoards information, and tasks get done quickly and efficiently. This is where the team truly *becomes* more than the sum of its parts.

Best if Left Alone

This category can seem controversial or even radical. It is based on the basic human truth that some problems solve themselves. You don't have to react to every email you receive and you don't need to give input on each and every corporate initiative that passes your desk. In today's age of constant, instant communication, information is shared much more broadly than in the past and than is often useful. Everyone gets emails that are addressed to entire corporate divisions. It's good information and it keeps you in the loop. It doesn't mean the CEO wants you to stop everything right then and start working to solve it. Rein in the urge to get involved in everything.

156

A DELICATE BALANCING ACT

A critical management decision can be determining how much time to spend on "nonproductive" work—meetings, conference calls, and other personal interaction—and how much time to spend on actually doing things. (Of course, they are not mutually exclusive.) It is an important balance: too much time on meetings and other "nonproductive" tasks takes away from actual output. But good communication and coordination relies on productive and frequent interaction of managers and employees at all levels. A manager who is lax about starting meetings on time, providing a clear agenda and purpose, and keeping things on course is not likely to achieve very desirable results and, in the long run, is likely to suffer from a performance and professional standpoint. A manager who is a stickler for punctual starts, keeps for the most part to the agenda, and limits "blue-sky" sidebars is not only much more likely to successfully execute on the project deliverables, but will also build professional equity with the project team members.

Handling interactions with people outside of meetings can turn into another balancing act because these usually bring some action item or response. To do it right requires a high degree of trust. Too many managers, for whatever reason, don't exhibit that trust and spend too much time on work their subordinates could and should handle. If these managers

157

delegate a task, they spend time valuable time looking over their employee's shoulder. If you trust your team, you'll rarely need to look over shoulders or spend too much time reviewing results. Tom, for example, trusts the people who report directly to him. More often than not, when he asks someone to communicate on his behalf, he doesn't add, "I want to see it first." It isn't laziness or time management on Tom's part. "It's just that I don't have to read it first. I trust them to do it right and send it to whoever needs to see it. They own their work and will stand up for it so I don't have to."

Interactions that are devoid of information development seldom are productive. Consider two different situations. In the first, the manager tells a direct report what he wants done, how he wants it done, and when it's due. No effort is made to solicit feedback from the person who'll be doing the task. It's a linear interaction. In the second case, the manager tells his direct report what needs to be done and asks her how she'll go about it. Her response may trigger an additional thought in his mind that might make the task easier or more useful. A short discussion occurs—mental Ping-Pong, Tom calls it—that leaves both the manager and the employee with a better understanding of how it will be done and why. The manager doesn't have to worry as much about whether it will be done right and the employee has a sense of confidence and self-worth that ensures she'll do her best to do the job right.

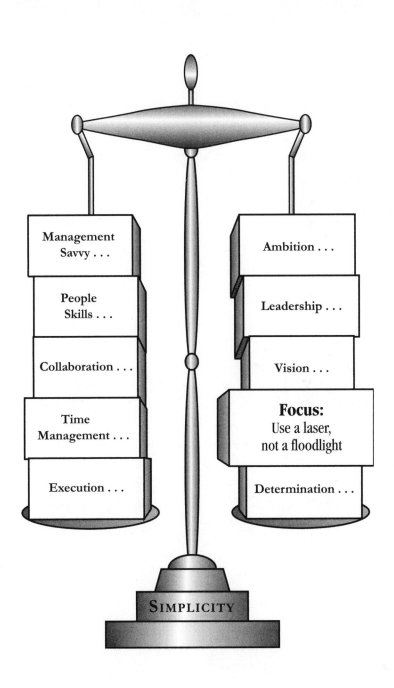

CHAPTER 9

Focus: Use a Laser, Not a Floodlight

Astonishing things can be done with the human memory if you will devote it faithfully to one particular line of business.

—Mark Twain, Life on the Mississippi

Think of the people who populate the executive suite in your company and one of the impressions that probably comes to mind is that they seem particularly good at focusing on a task, a goal, or a problem with a greater intensity than the general office population. Of course, one reason could be that the higher up you move, the more people you have employed to keep such distractions as telephones, visitors, and emails at bay. But true leaders do seem to have the ability to focus with laser-like clarity on whatever task is before them. They learn to manage time as a strategic resource, dividing the day, the week, the month or even the year into manageable chunks. They know how to delegate and leave themselves more time to do what they do best. Focus is the way to make the most use of each of those chunks of time. Focus is the right-brain complement to time management.

FOCUS ON GOALS

To focus on what matters, you need to actually *know* what matters. Tools are available to help, like the importance-urgency matrix we present in Chapter 6. But the essence of focus lies in tying everything back to goals—your company's overall goals, your division's goals, and your personal goals. Then ask yourself this question: Will focusing on this task or project or initiative have a real, measurable impact on reaching those goals? Another helpful concept is the Pareto Principle, or the 80/20 rule. This rule contends that in any given situation 80 percent of the solution lies in only 20 percent of the variables, or 80 percent of the problems are caused by 20 percent of the defects. According to this theory, if you can identify and focus on the variables that constitute that all-important 20 percent you can solve 80 percent of a problem. In 1906, Italian economist Vilfredo Pareto used his mathematical formula in describing how wealth was distributed in his country. In the 1940s, Dr. Joseph Juran, a management expert, applied a similar principle to quality when he wrote about "the vital few and trivial many." While Pareto applied the

80/20 rule to economics, Juran observed that 80 percent of the problems are caused by 20 percent of the
defects. It was Juran who made the 80/20 concept
one of the watchwords of management and ironically
it was through his writings that it came to be known
as the Pareto Principle. The American Society for
Quality has tried to get the Principle renamed the
"Juran Principle."

What are these key variables and how to we find
them? It's not as hard as it sounds—in fact, you and
your team can determine them by asking yourselves
a few simple questions. Here's an example of how
Tom does it: His division and others like it at FedEx
are often asked to develop strategic plans for a pre-
determined period of time. For our example, we'll
say three years. Tom and his team will boil down the
essence of the presentation to three key questions
that he and his staff must answer: Where do we need
to be in three years? Where are we now? How do we
get from where we are to where we need to be? With
that kind of simplification and the focus that results
from it, people can stay on target even when discussing targets that are three years away.

Most of us are capable of focusing to a much
greater degree than we usually do. Why is that? One
reason is that applying rigor and focus to your activities at work can be scary—it leaves very little "wriggle
room." Many people like to be very busy, multitasking

on several initiatives at once. That way if one project fails, it doesn't seem to matter that much, since you have so many other irons in the fire. Applying a greater focus can seem like "putting all your eggs in one basket." If you're clearly focused on a few high-impact goals, which you have clearly communicated to your superiors, you have just put a giant spotlight on your performance. That is what scares many people away from focus, but it's the courage to do so that separates out the great leaders.

FOCUS ON RESULTS

One very important element of focus is to keep your eye on results. That means focusing on the impact that activities, initiatives, and projects are intended to produce. Often, this requires digging a little deeper to define the problem at hand. For example, a customer might come to FedEx requesting a bid on 15 warehouse locations around the United States. As project manager, you may be tempted to jump immediately into a location analysis, finding the lowest bidders, and hammering together a transportation plan.

Stop!

What does this customer really want? The customer's number one need is the ability to deliver critical goods to key clients within 12 hours. Whether that means having 15 warehouses in place in strategic locations across the country may or may not be part of the answer. The right answer, however, just might be something else, perhaps the construction of two larger distribution centers on each coast coupled with the redesign of the customer's supply chain. Focusing on results means not jumping into action to give the customer—whether internal or external—exactly what they ask for. Instead, focus on what they really need. This takes courage because you may need to push back on over-eager constituents.

Sales Training at FedEx: Case Study

Until a few years ago, the FedEx sales training department was classroom-driven and the standard procedure was "training as an event"—fly sales professionals and managers to Memphis in shifts and bombard them with information and handouts.

As a project at FedEx involving several divisions was looking at the efficiency and effectiveness of the selling day, one of Tom's divisions was doing the same thing looking at the way FedEx educated its sales force. Time spent in Memphis was time spent *away* from customers. Lessons learned en masse in Memphis were not necessarily translating into more business, and some tests showed sales professionals weren't retaining much of the information, much less putting it to good use. Sales Training was about to be reborn as Sales Development and Education. As one of Tom's vice presidents was fond of saying, "We train dogs. We educate people."

Today, sales professionals have knowledge at their fingertips and the department is a world-class organization that educates with the goal of producing results. There is an extensive online catalog, a measurement and evaluation process, and a methodology that uses five different steps of evaluation.

Solutions teams worked together to design a long-term strategy for selling-skills reinforcement and made sure the newly hired sales professional and the veteran alike had the same foundation, or grounding, in how to sell the full FedEx portfolio. Sales Education built an all-encompassing coaching tool that provides a structured process to help managers develop their employees in the areas most needed.

Now when sales professionals complete their courses, their managers know what kinds of behavior to look for as a result. A checklist is provided by Sales Education and Development and within a few weeks of the course completion date, the managers use it to evaluate whether or not the employees are using the skills and techniques learned in classes.

Sales professionals began to see an emphasis on selling the value of FedEx rather than "our price versus their price" and Sales Education and Development teams began providing the courses to back up that strategy.

Sales professionals no longer get their information spoon-fed to them. Instead, Tom's division adopted the "teach a man to fish and he'll never go hungry" way of thinking. The FedEx sale teams know how to get the right information themselves and they can do it on their own timetable. They get new or refresher information as they need it and when they need it.

FOCUS ON COMMUNICATION

Learning to focus on results is a necessary but not sufficient condition of becoming a great leader. It needs to be supplemented by focused communication. Your best, most focused, and rigorous work cannot have the impact it should if you cannot communicate in a focused way. When you take on a new, complex project or division or initiative, the number of things that need to be communicated can quickly seem overwhelming. Your first step needs to be to filter out the extraneous parts—what is the essence and what is noise around it?

One way to get to the essence is to ask very simple questions, keeping in mind the KISS principle (Keep It Simple, Stupid). Examples include: What is this division trying to do? What problem are we trying to solve? Why hasn't this worked in the past? What is the one thing we need to get right?

Simple questions will help you develop simple structures around your problem or project. If you remember from an earlier chapter, simplicity is at the core of this book. Boiling things down to their essence and then communicating this essence is the hallmark of a great leader. Simple questions and simple structures help you do this. Too often, managers try to look "smart" by applying complex analysis and business-school constructs to a problem. Strong leaders are not afraid to use simple, straightforward thinking to tackle difficult issues. And whether it's in an executive boardroom or a manager's staff meeting, listeners applaud the presenter who makes his message clear, concise, and immediately understandable.

Communications that are focused are closely tied to clarity of thinking. It is nearly impossible to construct simple, focused communications around an issue without the ability to break complex issues down into simple questions. Do you have clarity of thinking on your project's message? Can you summarize the essence of it in one or two sentences? Is your story logical? Could you explain what you're doing to a 12-year-old? This is the kind of communicating that sets you apart as a leader.

FOCUS ON VALUE

Tom keeps focused on the right things by applying the "Leave a place better than you found it" principle to every interaction, whether it is at work or in his personal life. Every day, you have dozens of interactions and in every one of them you make a conscious or unconscious choice to either add or not add value. "I may have eight to ten face-to-face meetings, dozens of scheduled and unscheduled phone calls, and more emails than I want to remember," Tom explains. "I try very hard to make every single one of these interactions count: to leave the email sender, the project team members I am meeting with, or the customer on the phone in a better situation by virtue of our conversation. It does take extra effort, but the payoff is so much bigger for all involved."

That's why you'll never get a mere acknowledgment email from Tom—he'll have something valid to say, or he won't say anything.

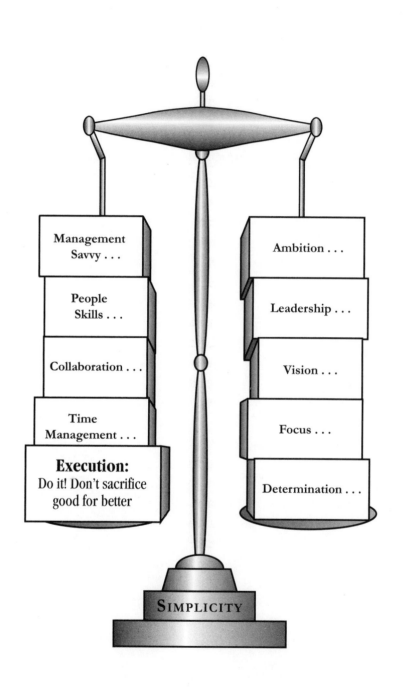

CHAPTER 10

Execution: Do It! Don't Sacrifice Good for Better

Do, or do not. There is no "try."

—Yoda, *The Empire Strikes Back*

Nike's famous slogan, "Just Do It," has been one of the most successful marketing phrases of all time. It embodies in the simplest form the underlying attitude required to successfully run a business. Great leaders know the value of analysis, of designing strategy and involving all constituents. But they also have a knack for realizing when it's time to act, to go and "just do it." Execution is the skill of getting things off the drawing board and into action. Execution is also inherent in keeping things going and staying on course, so it's only natural that this tool is paired with the passion of determination. Determination is the underlying passion that keeps you and your team executing when things get tough. How you execute, how you stay on target and measure results, and how and when you change course are all critical aspects of running your operation and making your team the best it can be. The point of execution, of course, is to reach the goals set for your team. Yet execution seldom goes smoothly. Invariably crises—unplanned and unpredictable events—arise to divert us from execution. That's when determination becomes a vital component of our ability to execute well.

CREATING A CULTURE OF EXECUTION

Tom and Arnold have years of experience in devising and executing business and civic plans, and both believe that good execution begins with a bias toward action. They know that waiting too long can be fatal to a project since no one ever has all the information they need or want at the beginning. And, by the time you get around to that last little bit of data, the conditions under which you began the project will more than likely have changed and will need to be re-evaluated. This repetition of waiting and re-evaluation is commonly known as "analysis paralysis." Managers who become trapped in this stage are still reading and writing reports, trying to decide what to do while their competitors have new and innovative products in development or on the way to market. Instilling a "bias for action" in your team is the antidote for "analysis paralysis." It means modeling execution by not asking for one more report or analysis, but by moving forward decisively with sufficient, albeit often incomplete, information.

It means throwing something against the wall to see if it sticks. Put something—anything—on paper to get the ball rolling.

To be biased toward action, you need to be willing to take a few risks. Because you don't spend exhaustive time studying the problem, analyzing, doing focus groups, and writing reports, there's a chance you will make mistakes. But even if you make a mistake, the fact that you're out of the gate ahead of everyone else leaves you plenty of time to fix it, to make mid-course corrections, and remain ahead of the pack. Chances are, however, that your decision will be at least 80 percent right, that your team will be energized with excitement and that the competition will be left behind studying data while you're solving problems and seizing opportunities. There's an old axiom that captures this bias toward action: "Ask for forgiveness, not permission." People who work for true leaders know it's okay to make a few mistakes. That's what empowers them to take risks.

Taking these risks makes good business sense, a point that many managers forget as they wallow in the details of a proposal and wind up incurring hidden costs through delay. Even though spending extra time upfront might seem the safe and most fiscally responsible way to operate, waiting has a potentially high cost, commonly known in business and finance as "opportunity costs."

Good execution takes place in two steps. The first is getting things off the ground. The second is keeping the momentum going and keeping the project on course.

Being Directionally Correct

Many of FedEx's customers ask for help in redesigning their supply chains for maximum efficiency. For big companies with lots of products to distribute, this can be critically important as well as a huge change. Multiple considerations come into play—the number and locations of warehouses, the modes of transportation, the variety of products and the changing demand for those products. Once you start factoring variables into an equation, things can get complicated very quickly. The fact is there will never be enough time or information to help you arrive at the perfect answer. Anyone who tries to devise one will spend the next several years running models, while his competitor is helping the customer redesign his supply chain.

The key to helping the customer solve the problem is to set the extreme parameters and use analysis to migrate toward the sweet spot, a more immediate solution, which often tends to be somewhere close to the middle of two extremes. The "right" answer can be one that is "directionally correct." In other words, the solution may not be perfect (no one else's will be, either), but it's in the ballpark. This paves the way for more action but at least you're already working with the customer and aren't stuck back at the starting gate, still refining the model in the search for the non-existent "perfect" solution.

Good execution is like flying an airplane. Airplanes don't travel in a straight line from point A to point B. Pilots start off heading in the general direction of their destination and then constantly make small corrections—changes in speed and direction—to "get back on course."

The Fast Track Approach to Design and Construction

FedExForum is an example of applying this principle in a large project setting. The state-of-the-art arena in Memphis got built on time and on budget. The construction industry calls this process "fast track." Years ago the design and construction of a building took place in carefully sequenced steps. An architect first executed a set of drawings to be approved by the owner. Once the design process was over, the completed plans were turned over to the contractors who then built the building. The fast-track approach saves time and money by combining those two formerly distinctive steps. The overall outlines of the building are drawn and turned over to the contractors, who begin construction even before the final drawings are complete. To an outsider it appears to be a risky proposition: what if you forget something, like an elevator shaft or a stairwell? Are you then back to square one? Of course not—you can address these issues later in the process. And given the huge opportunity cost involved in every delay, it makes sense to take that additional risk.

HYPOTHESIS-DRIVEN WORK

As a manager, you can devise your own fast-track approach to undertaking new initiatives or solving problems. You begin it by writing your final project presentation the day you begin it. In other words, you articulate where you're going before you even leave the gate. You develop hypotheses around your end product, defined as the desired outcome. You won't have precise details and won't know exactly how the end result will look, but you will be able to produce a series of headlines about various major steps toward your goal. The trick is not to become so wedded to your hypotheses that you're in danger of making foregone conclusions without any evidence. A device that can help visualize the end result is the storyboard, something that television and movie producers use to set up the sequence of scenes in a program. By storyboarding your hypotheses, you will drive the work in an actionable way while still being open to needed revisions. Here's how a storyboard would work if you were given the assignment to develop a new method of marketing financial services to young adults.

The first step is to state your initial hypothesis. In this case, it might be something like "Young adults are not focusing sufficiently on their financial needs." To prove or disprove that hypothesis, you will look for specific data on that subject. But even before you begin to research that topic, you can state a few more hypotheses. One might be that "young people do not respond to traditional marketing methods." If you assume for the moment that your second hypothesis is correct, it would then lead to another hypothesis: "Young adults respond best to marketing that has certain characteristics." You don't yet know what those characteristics are, but you will find out in the course of this project. Yet another hypothesis might be this: "The most successful ways other services companies reach young adults are: (again, you don't know the answer, but you know you'll want to find out)." A final hypothesis might be this: "We can apply some of these best practices by . . ." Now you have a tentative outline of where you want to go and what you need to know to get there. It's not a problem if one of your hypotheses turns out to be wrong. All you need do is start another storyboard at that point with a new set of hypotheses.

TOOLS AND TIMELINES

Execution often begins by breaking a project down into separate parts that can be placed on a timeline. The timeline is important for setting up the sequence of events that have to happen to reach your ultimate goal. But not every aspect of a project has to be done sequentially. You'll grab plenty of the low-hanging fruit along the way, freeing people and resources to focus on the more difficult aspects of the project.

It's important to keep your team focused on producing actionable recommendations instead of continually raising issues or concerns, getting input or doing analysis. One way to ensure that a team stays focused on action is SMART goals. The acronym stands for goals that are Specific, Measurable, Attainable, Realistic, and Tangible. Goals with these characteristics will greatly simplify execution. A SMART goal is specific. It makes a clear statement ("we *will* bring a new detergent product to market by June 1, 2007"), not just a vague notion. A SMART goal is measurable. It might be the number of new customers or the increase in revenues. If you can't devise a way to measure it, chances are your goal isn't formulated properly. SMART goals are attainable and realistic. They aren't so far off the charts that they are really just pipe dreams. Finally, SMART goals are tangible, clear, and firmly linked to the bottom line.

184

STAYING ON COURSE

Once you launch a project, it's easy to lose some of the energy and excitement that accompanied the kickoff. Yet it is crucial at this stage to maintain focus, to be determined to complete the job, and to keep the team's stamina and enthusiasm high. Though we all hate them, deadlines are a key tool in that process. Without specific deadlines, things simply don't get done. Remember the "Urgent/Important" chart from Chapter 8. Without deadlines to keep you focused, only the "urgent and important" and "urgent but not important" categories would get your attention. The headlines that you wrote at the beginning of the project can be useful as deadlines, too. They provide incremental and sequential checkpoints that help ensure that you're making the necessary progress.

Sustaining the team's enthusiasm and stamina, especially during a lengthy project, is one of the more difficult challenges facing you as a manager. Some projects (for example continuous improvement initiatives), are never complete. The deadlines you set based on the headlines you wrote can provide occasions for celebration and reenergizing the team, but there will sometimes be long stretches of time when there isn't an obvious reason for celebration. That's when you make up one. A self-defined milestone is better than none and allows the team to celebrate progress to date.

When FedEx began taking a long hard look at the efficiency and effectiveness of its sales force, it required a large project team made up of analysts, project managers, database experts, technology experts, pricing teams, marketing departments, communicators—nearly every division in FedEx's newly created Services division. Team members ranged from the newly hired to the executive.

The project, dubbed Zenith, would be spread out over multiple years and delivered in multiple phases. Simplicity was the key as divisions began analyzing things like selling time, barriers to selling, sales segments, and getting the right information into the sales professionals' hands *before* the visit to the customer. How many calls were sales professionals making in a day? Was the route used in making those calls mapped in a logical way, or were reps zigzagging around their territories wasting time and fuel? Which customers were called on by which sales division? Did the assignments make sense? But what is the best way to align accounts to sales segments? How long does it take sales employees to get the revenue and volume and performance reports they need? Are the right reports even available?

The project generated intense energy when it was first launched, but after more than a year it was obvious the energy was waning. Resources had to be divided between the two major areas at the forefront of the project: the "business" owners and the IT owners. Competing priority lists, timelinesn and changing specifications caused more than one budget tug-of-war. Employees on the front lines of Zenith began to lose sight of the goal and many felt they were spinning their wheels on something that would never reap rewards. Many of the teams had no direct contact or relationship with the sales teams and had only a vague idea of what sales reps' jobs entailed.

It was clear that some sort of reinvigoration was needed and fast. A team in Tom's division began assessing what had already been accomplished, the benefits already in place, and what was just over the horizon. Sales professionals and managers taped video segments, offering testimonials about what Zenith had already done for them and how excited they were about upcoming wins. Each video testimonial ended with a heartfelt, "Thank you, Zenith teams!" A FedEx auditorium was filled to capacity as executives from all the divisions came together to thank the teams for their hard work and celebrate their successes, their wins completed and those still to come. Sales professionals and executives alike stood on the stage and said, "Here's what we used to have, and here's what we have now. Thank you, Zenith teams." There were balloons, banners, and everything short of a marching band. Everyone got a T-shirt, a reception, and a sincere pat on the back and too many "thanks" to count.

The "Zenith Reinvigoration" accomplished what it set out to do. It said "thank you" to a lot of people for a lot of hard work and it celebrated milestones. One of its key successes, however, was letting many of the teams know just what their work was accomplishing in the real world. Writing intricate code and building a system that works is a win in and of itself. But when the coder hears how this new system provided information in a way that shaved an hour of time off a sales professional's day, it's an even bigger win. And when the techies and the analysts hear firsthand just how much revenue is being added to the company's coffers because of this new way of doing business, it sends an important message. Most important it said: "You are making an impact; you are making jobs easier; you are helping the company be more successful. You are doing a stellar job, and it is not going unnoticed."

Other helpful tools in keeping things going are progress reviews with senior management. We often think these are mainly done to keep senior management informed, but they are just as important in getting exposure and buy-in from senior management and keeping the team excited. Nothing rallies the troops like knowing that their work is being reviewed and recognized by the CEO.

Scorecards are a great way to monitor progress, especially in long-term projects. SMART goals that are measurable make it easy to devise a scorecard to do the measuring. A scorecard can also act as a warning mechanism when things get off track.

SANITY CHECKS

There is a fine line between execution and stubbornness. Some managers become so driven, singularly focused on action, and executing against plan that they fail to see that the plan may have become obsolete. Despite a "bias for action" it is important to take a timeout for sanity checks along the way to make sure the path you're on is still headed in the right direction. This is where input and reviews from outside your team can be especially helpful. Consider presenting your progress to an executive from another part of your company, or an outside consultant, to get a clear view from someone who is not mired in the execution.

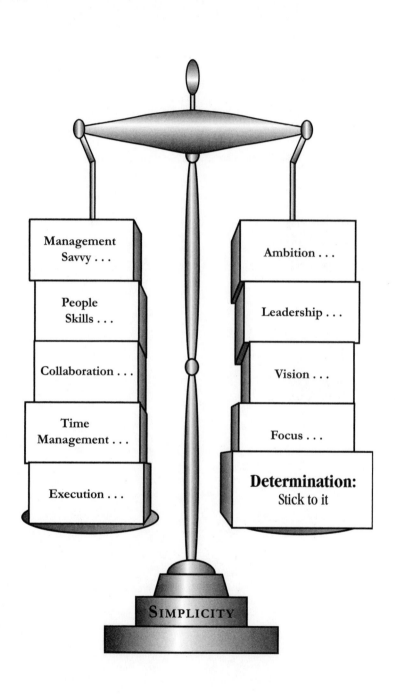

CHAPTER **11**

Determination: Stick to It

Swing hard, in case they throw the ball where you're swinging.

—Duke Snider

A chieving goals that are worth achieving requires effort. We set most goals with the knowledge of some of the hurdles we'll have to clear to achieve them. But invariably hurdles we didn't see at first arise along the way, making it even more difficult to get where we're going. Determination—the will to accomplish a goal, especially in the face of difficulties—is one of the most valuable passions a manager can have.

A "CAN-DO" ATTITUDE

Determination often manifests itself in a "can-do" attitude that looks for ways to do things rather than looking for reasons something won't work. Tom has always admired and aspired to that attitude. Growing up in Germany, he would often listen to the American Armed Forces Network. It was the venerable disc jockey Casey Kasem, with his upbeat "reach for the stars" optimism, who first made a young Tom Schmitt aspire to become a part of that American spirit. Over the years, Tom's admiration and respect for America continued to grow. When he took a job with British Petroleum in London years later, he jockeyed to get an assignment with an American executive who would be going back to the United States in a year or two and who promised to take Tom with him.

"After college I was even more determined to become part of the American 'can do' versus a 'can't do' world," he recalls. "It was my fundamental belief early on that Americans had a determination and cultural attitude to make things work."

Tom wanted to work with people who got things done, not people who could always come up with a dozen reasons something couldn't be done. Surrounding yourself with a team of "can-do" determined people instead a bunch of naysayers will enable you to reach stretch goals together.

The determination to stick to a course of action in the face of obstacles requires that you believe in what you are doing. From time to time, check your inner compass and follow your heart. If what needs to be executed still feels right, find three different ways to make it happen; don't accept the five reasons why it can't.

THE POWER OF INTENTION

"If you can dream it, you can do it" is a motto frequently utilized by top athletes to harness the power of visualization to generate peak performance—to create their statement of intent. An intention is a well-formulated, succinct, and clear statement of what you want to achieve. This is the opposite of a vague "good intention." Formulating clear intentions and then communicating those to your team, your boss, and your collaborators within your organization allows you to harness your energy and theirs around your goal.

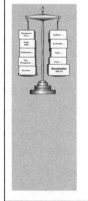

Intention Examples

✔ We will double our revenue this year.
✔ We will serve 200 new clients this quarter.
✔ We will find a marketing strategy to penetrate this new customer segment.
✔ We will cut costs per service call to $x this year.
✔ We will provide online training on all of our products to all of our salespeople by 200X.

DETERMINATION VERSUS DISTRACTIONS

Determination is the willingness and ability to overcome obstacles. Good managers use their own business savvy and the talents and efforts of their teams to identify, diagnose, and solve problems as they arise in the business environment. How well you do that may depend in large measure on how intractable a problem appears to be. Most people are willing to make an effort to solve easy problems, but far fewer are willing to devote the mental effort, energy, and time to solving the more complex ones.

The second characteristic of a determined manager is the ability to avoid distraction. Faced with a worrisome situation that requires extraordinary efforts to fix it, some managers decide simply to find something else to do. Their hope, seldom realized, is that the difficult problem will just go away. With many items on your plate, it is easy to become distracted by problems on one issue, or a more pressing agenda on others. Determination requires continued focus and commitment to a project. It requires the business savvy to separate the core of an issue from ancillary matters and then to continue plugging away at the core.

However, it is also important to know when determination turns into stubbornness. We've all known managers who were unwilling to let go of pet projects even in the face of fundamental changes. This is why determination is an art. It requires walking a fine line between passionate focus and blind stubbornness. Determination can be futile and frustrating if it is directed at the wrong goals. When you run into a seemingly insurmountable wall a second and third time, it might be time to stop for a moment and reconsider your goal. Is it really the right goal? If it is, why are you having such trouble keeping on a course to reach it? Flexibility is an important part of every manager's psychological makeup. Use your judgment to determine if the goal needs to be simplified, changed, or even abandoned altogether. Don't confuse sheer stubbornness with determination.

DETERMINED TEAMS

The third trait of determination is the ability to generate and keep yourself and your team energetic and enthused about the job and the challenges. How do you get a group of people determined to achieve success? It takes selecting the right people for the project, setting clear common goals, and instilling enthusiasm and pride for the project. Making goals public, for example, in a company newsletter or at a divisional meeting, is one way of generating team energy. Making goals public has a way of increasing our determination because we want to avoid the shame of failure. It also helps to persuade other constituents, such as other departments or customers, to become allies in helping us achieve our goals.

A "can-do" determined attitude is not a mindset you acquire once and for all. Working on complex, long-term goals requires ongoing re-fueling of energy, both for yourself and your team.

Be Part of the Solution, Not the Problem

Anthropologists tell us that humans are predisposed to resist change. As humans, we tend to prefer the status quo over difficult renewal. Determination is how you overcome that resistance to change. A determined team is composed of people who are focused on jointly developing solutions, not naysayers who try to debunk solutions without offering alternatives. As a leader, you need to hold accountable people who exhibit that kind of negativity: They're only allowed to voice doubts about a course of action if they can propose a reasonable alternative. In other words, they have to be part of the solution, not part of the problem.

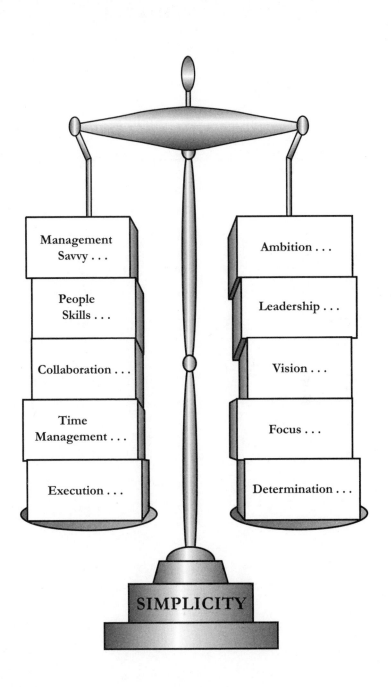

CHAPTER 12

Keep It Simple!

There is no greatness where simplicity, goodness and truth are absent.

—Leo Tolstoy

As you're now well aware, our approach to leadership involves the careful balancing of tools and passions built on the foundation of simplicity. We particularly like McKenzie's approach to simplicity: "All good things come in threes." So here are our three takeaways from *Simple Solutions:*

1. Keep it simple.
2. Keep your tools and passions in balance.
3. Become a disciple of *Simple Solutions.*

THE VALUE OF SIMPLICITY

Simplicity isn't always easy to achieve, but the benefits *are* always worth the effort. You can feel the power of simplicity when you take a complicated problem and carefully reduce it to the basics that make it is easy for you not only to understand, but also to communicate to others. The simple Red Card that drove the management of the immensely complex FedExForum arena project is a real-life example of what can be accomplished by simplifying, evangelizing, and collaborating.

When you think about the value of simplicity, you begin to see evidence of it all around you. Consider the real estate mantra that we've all heard over the years: "Location, location, location." That's the simple solution to the challenge of purchasing what probably is the single-most-expensive object most of us will ever own.

At FedEx, of course, the mantra is "People, Service, Profit." That simple phrase, which is the DNA of the company, was Smith's concept for the company that created an entirely new industry in 1973.

If your job puts you in the spotlight, you might wind up working with a media consultant to help you prepare for interviews. The first thing your consultant will tell you is "keep it simple." You'll have three messages to convey when you begin the interview, and, regardless of the questions asked, those are the messages that you will repeat to make your points memorable for the audience.

The Value of Simplicity

If you've ever glanced in the cockpit of an airliner as you board, you almost certainly have wondered how the pilots make any sense of the hundreds of switches, gauges, dials, and displays. It's simple. They focus on the things that are especially critical to their aircraft: flight direction, air speed, altitude, rate of climb, and fuel. You practice the same focus in your car; you often check your speed, but don't constantly check the oil pressure gauge, the radio dial, or the window controls. That's why you think driving is "simple." If you spend a little time riding with a novice driver, you see that a learner doesn't find this focus as simple. When you learn what's important, it can become "simple."

Simplification isn't an end unto itself. Rather, it becomes a means of communication. As an attorney, Arnold and his colleagues, who present cases before the United States Court of Appeals, understand the concepts of simplicity and communication. The court customarily allows each party only 15 minutes to present oral arguments and answer questions. If you can't reduce your argument to a few principle arguments (or messages), you generally end up losing. A shotgun approach simply doesn't work. You need a laser or a rifle approach with no more than three pieces of ammo.

Similarly, a manager in the workplace needs to simplify his or her message to the workforce. In most employee opinion surveys taken by companies in the private sector, the quality of corporate communication is generally ranked lower by employees than even wages or benefits. Why? In many instances, it is caused by an inattention to effective communication. It's as important to be as focused and easy to understand when you communicate with your employees as it would be if you were a lawyer presenting your arguments to a United States Court of Appeals.

Amid all the complexities of modern business, it is sometimes tough not to get bogged down in details and complexity. Norman Vincent Peale, who influenced lives around the world, explained that "we struggle with the complexities and avoid the simplicities." We admire leaders who can provide focus by boiling down complex problems to their simplest proportions. If you become a disciple of *Simple Solutions,* you can become adept at this core management technique.

A SENSE OF BALANCE

When we first began to think about the similarity of our management styles, we both were struck by our "right-brain, left-brain" model of analysis and creativity and turned that model into our tools and passions. Only later did we also realize that good managers and exceptional leaders need to achieve a "balance" between the two sides. That's when we conceived of the balance scale as the embodiment of our leadership philosophy.

We've all heard horror stories about how certain managers are nothing more than "technocrats," who lack any semblance of people skills. Fairly or unfairly, professionals in engineering, accounting, and information technology too often are regarded as being predominantly "left-brain people." Conversely, other professionals, who sometimes have backgrounds in only nontechnical fields, fail to receive the respect they deserve because they are viewed as "right-brain people." There's certainly some validity in those stereotypes, and if you tend to be over-balanced toward one side or the other of the scale, you need to make adjustments to bring your management skills into balance. It isn't hard to get a sense of your balance using such devices as 360-degree reviews or even self-assessments. To keep their licenses current, pilots have to undergo check rides in simulators or in actual flight. As a manager and leader, you need to undertake a personal "check ride" every so often to make sure your leadership scale is well balanced.

SIMPLE SOLUTIONS LEAD TO REMARKABLE RESULTS

If you've read *Simple Solutions* from cover to cover, you now are armed with the necessary tools and information that allow you to become proactive and put your own personal plan for leadership growth in place. Remember, it isn't a sprint; it's a marathon. Enjoy the process but crave the goal. Maybe you want to make your own personal laminated "strategy card." However you do it, just remember to keep it simple. Albert Einstein expressed it this way with his three rules of work: "Out of clutter find simplicity; from discord find harmony; in the middle of difficulty lies opportunity."

After you've read *Simple Solutions,* ask yourself this question: Does the acronym KISS really make sense? If you agree with the underlying thesis of this book, wouldn't it make more sense to change the Keep it simple, "Stupid" into Keep it simple . . . *Smarty?* After all, there is nothing stupid about keeping it simple!

We share a passion for accomplishment through teamwork. The tools and passions we present in this book are the keys that set in motion the process of hardwiring your brain for results and engaging the hearts and minds of those around you to get the results you need. We sincerely believe that if you adopt and implement these *Simple Solutions,* you stand the best chance of making tomorrow better than today.

Simplicity is the final achievement. After one has played a vast quantity of notes and more notes, it is simplicity that emerges as the crowning reward of art.

—Frederic Chopin

Index

Index

Index